WHEN A LITTLE ONE HUMS

My Journey of Healing from Childhood
Trauma Through Listening Prayer

WHEN A LITTLE ONE HUMS

My Journey of Healing from Childhood Trauma Through Listening Prayer

F. T. DAVIDSON

Illustrated by Destiny Loeve

Copyright © 2021 F. T. Davidson

All rights reserved. No part of this publication may be reproduced, distributed, or transmitted in any form or by any means, without prior written permission from the author, except brief excerpts for review purposes.

ISBN: 9798473501643

Dedication

To the memory of my Little Fi's.
You who I was once so ashamed of have become my pride and joy.
Thank you for teaching me who I am.

Contents

Foreword	9
Before We Begin	11
Part 1: The Journey	**13**
Introduction	15
How to Use This Book	25
The Cave: An Invitation to Maturity	27
Into the Silence	33
Part 2: The Little Ones	**41**
Hidden One	43
The Unaffirmed Ones	49
Fetus Fi	57
Can a Statue Cry?	63
The Bruised One	67
The Invisible One and the Burden Express	73
The Insignificant Ones	83
The Uncertain One	93
The Helping Ones (Little Mother and Gentle One)	101
Hopeless One	105
The Intimidated One	115
The Lake of Sorrows	119
Meeting the Twins	129
Traumatized One (Part 1)	135
Traumatized One (Part 2)	139

Brave Front 145

PART 3: AFTERTHOUGHTS **155**
The Great Allower and the
   Great Co-Sufferer 157
Trauma and Listening Prayer 163
Comments on Listening Prayer:
   Eden Jersak 165
Comments on Listening Prayer:
   Lorie Martin 169
Epilogue 171

Foreword

In the pages of this book you will read intimately about Fiona's remarkable healing journey experienced through Listening Prayer, a way of praying that opens one to encounter Jesus and hear his voice. In each time of prayer, Jesus beautifully meets Fiona where she is at on her journey and tenderly offers what she needs for healing and transformation. Consistently, we witness Jesus's boundless love and limitless grace, compassion, and kindness. Through Fiona's experiences with Jesus, we are reminded of and discover anew who Jesus is. To read this unique offering of a book is to read a modern-day gospel story.

I have the joy today of knowing Fiona and watching as she leads many other hearts to encounter God through Listening Prayer. It reminds me of Jesus's words, "Freely you have received, freely give." Out of her transformation, Fiona invites others to encounter Jesus and experience their own metamorphosis.

I have been experiencing and facilitating Listening Prayer since 2004. Encountering Jesus through this prayer practice has transformed my life. I have also had the honour of companioning many others as they encounter God intimately and experience healing and freedom. Today

I have the joy of training others in facilitating Listening Prayer. As you read this book, it is my hope that you too will encounter Jesus in your heart and life and that you will experience Jesus offering you healing, love, compassion, and kindness. May God do more than you could ask or imagine!

Katherine Murray (2021)

Before We Begin

I am completely comfortable with God as both the Masculine Divine and the Feminine Divine, and I am grateful for this season of my life where I can explore all that this means. I can finally recognize my own womanly likeness in God, and if you and I were chatting face to face, I might sometimes speak of God as "she." However, for the sake of simplicity and in order not to distract from the essence of what I wish to share in my writing here, I will refer to God as the traditional "he."

You will notice in my writing that I speak of parts of me that didn't seem able to grow up, still stuck in the wounds and traumas of my childhood. These were my embarrassing immaturities that I might at one time have labelled as my weaknesses or even my sinful nature. It became much easier to work with them once I started to see them as younger child parts of myself rather than just difficult, unwanted emotions and reactions. This way I could visualize a real child, a young Fi, and I could dialogue with her. Relating to a living child evoked compassion in me and a desire to help her and care for her. Over time I came to affectionately call these parts of myself my "inner children," my "Little Fi's" and my "Little Ones," which you will see frequently referenced in the pages that follow.

I am not a trained counselor, therapist, psychiatrist, or psychologist, and I have no interest in trying to diagnose myself. Nor am I advocating that Listening Prayer is the only pathway to healing or that everyone will experience it as I did. What I share with you is simply my personal story. I cannot speak for anyone else.

Part 1
THE JOURNEY

Introduction

I first learned about Listening Prayer in 2003 when I, my then husband, and our two small boys emigrated to Canada from Britain. Our new church, a community called Freshwind, practiced this type of prayer as a natural part of everyday life. I had always loved the Old Testament way more than the New, largely because of the conversations so many Old Testament folks had with our invisible God. I was drawn to those dialogues and exchanges and wondered why we had lost the art of this form of natural communication in the centuries since Christ had come. Nowadays, hearing from God seemed to be largely limited to his speaking through the Scriptures, the pastor, or "signs from above" and synchronicities that showed us that we were being "led by God." I wanted more, a back-and-forth conversation with a real, living Spiritual Being, and not just about direction and purpose!

Listening Prayer, I quickly learned, was not afraid of the imagination. I have always been quite a visual person; perhaps that is why it was such a good fit for me. It allowed me to explore and embrace the pictures that floated through my mind, the moving images that surfaced on the screen of my imagination, and I could invite the living

Jesus into them and literally watch what he did and listen to what he said. I figured he may be nothing more than a genie conjured up by my brain's grey matter, but the extraordinary thing was that he turned out to be dynamically different from how I had imagined God to be, and my journey with Listening Prayer held many wonderful and unexpected surprises as I got to "know" him. What's more, I am convinced that the process began to alter my neural pathways, and over time I found myself more and more liberated from the effects of my traumatic childhood.

It is not necessary for this book that I share many details of my growing-up years. The stories you will read later in these pages will tell you enough. But I think it is fair to say that I am what is called today a "super-feeler," and being highly sensitive as a child made our tumultuous home life quite overwhelming for me. I do think I was a difficult first-born for my mother in particular—a very complex and needy woman whose behaviors I can only really understand now through the lens of mental illness and the knowledge that she had survived a troubled childhood herself. She and my father were well educated and full of noble passions and ideas but not necessarily equipped for parenthood. Sadly, I have no happy memories of my first eighteen years, except for the short holidays with my grandfather each summer when my parents were not with us. Undoubtedly, this was not because there weren't any fun and beautiful family moments, but my brain was so consumed with anxiety, fear, and distress that I could not seem to hold onto them. I lived with constant dread in my belly, a permanent sensation that my body then normalized. As an adult I wished I could forget my past, but it haunted me, and I was forever being triggered by God knows what! By the time I was in my forties, it had become a wearisome nightmare to which there seemed no end. I felt like I was constantly playing whack-a-mole as bits and pieces from my early years, including weird attitudes and reactions, popped up uninvited from within myself during my day-to-day interactions. Oh boy, it was exhausting trying to keep it all under control! Plus, it was embarrassing since it blatantly contradicted the kind of person I felt I was supposed to be (and desperately wanted to be) as a practicing Christian. I had attended counselling in Britain over different periods of time, but the results were disappointing. The whole thing felt pointless, as none of the counselors seemed to know how to help me.

You can only imagine the spark of hope I felt when I heard the Freshwind pastor, Brad Jersak, inviting us to participate in various Listening Prayer exercises each Sunday and acknowledging so matter-of-factly that younger "parts" of us may sometimes show up in the encounter. Everything in me strained toward this glimmer of light. Could it be that I might finally start to make some sense of myself? And could it be that there might be help for someone like me, trapped in a prison of inner torment?

Another pastor, Lorie Martin, arrived at the church a month after we did, and she began to head up all aspects of prayer ministry and training, including Listening Prayer. I signed up immediately, and within a short period of time Lorie and Brad's wife, Eden, began to meet regularly with me. It was the beginning of a journey that was to take three and a half years and more Listening Prayer sessions than I would care to count.

I do not know what persuaded them to labour through with me or to keep agreeing to meet with me again and again. I don't think there was much about me to endear me to them at that time, and although each prayer time ended on a positive note, it was only a matter of hours before my next "issue" surfaced. I was afraid that I was a drain on their time and energy as my painful story just didn't seem to get better.

For the final six months another pastor couple took over to give Lorie and Eden a break, and then, as if by magic, the polluted, gushing rivers of my childhood pain simply dried up. The last dregs had been wrung out, and there was nothing left but the chance to inhale the entirely new sensation of freedom from dread. Finally, I was able to start to step away from my past and consider myself as "woman" rather than child, as survivor instead of victim.

I will never be able to repay the debt of gratitude I owe all these dear folks or the Freshwind community who embraced and carried me through those years with true unconditional love. They literally facilitated a miracle, marking a watershed point on the journey of my life, from which there is only the life before, and the life after.

In the early days of our Listening Prayer sessions, it became quickly apparent to Lorie that the clamor for attention of my younger parts was going to need some kind of orderly system if things were not to get out of hand. She asked Brad if he would help us build a safehouse in my heart in which all my Little Ones could live under Christ's rule and care. I had spent my entire life trying to suppress and alienate my fractured childish parts and had certainly never made any attempt to befriend them or care for their needs. I considered them my enemies; I hated myself, every part of me. So, when I tried to imagine where they might be found, I discovered they were scattered far and wide, as far away from me as they could manage, in what I described then as "hellholes."

Brad's job was to help me create an internal safehouse using my imagination (which we referred to at that time as the House of the Lord) and then facilitate the transference there of all my Little Ones, from the dark hiding places where they presently resided. I pictured a large, white three-story mansion surrounded by spacious gardens and a walled perimeter for security. The entrance to the house had four tall pillars across a wide porch. Inside was a grand curving polished wood staircase leading up to the next floor where there were bedrooms, nurseries, and playrooms for all the children. On the top floor were rooms with softly padded walls where the most damaged (and harmful) of my inner children were to be looked after. The most significant room of the house was on the ground floor, a meeting room where the children could be interviewed by Jesus and me when they were ready. We called this the Kindness Room because it was a place where kindness prevailed, and where there was no need for fear. It surprised me that its walls were red. This did not seem very relaxing to me, nor would it have been my colour choice, but I also noticed a vase of lovely yellow daffodils on a table in front of one of the windows, which brightened the place up nicely. The Kindness Room had a large open fireplace in which a fire often burned. It smelled quite wonderful and could be enjoyed from the comfy couch positioned in front of it. There was only one rule in this house, unconditional love.

I remember the day the safehouse was set up. Listening Prayer was always an embarrassing process for me because I was self-conscious and ashamed to uncover my inner immaturity. I was also hyper-sensitive about taking up other peoples' valuable time. This was one of those days, but I knew it was important, so I pressed on anyway. I think our prayer time only took about thirty minutes. In my mind's eye I saw Little Ones gathered in from the farthest reaches of the universe to the hostile wastelands of the Arctic, to dark, festering underground caverns. Once I sensed they were all in, the door of the house was shut, and a strange quiet overtook me, the stillness of stunned children suddenly uprooted and then opening their eyes to a new environment that was so remarkably different from what they had ever known before. They made no sound as they tried to take in this place of safety, comfort, and peace. This peculiar feeling stayed with me for a few days and was altogether welcome. The healing had begun!

From then on our prayer ministry times generally took place in the Kindness Room: Jesus, adult Fi, and a Little One, as you will read in the stories that follow. I let God decide who we would meet next rather than trying to navigate in a particular direction. Truth be told, whichever child part of me was making the most nuisance of herself was usually the one we met at our next appointment! They had a way of surfacing from my subconscious and drawing attention to themselves, their thoughts and messages, their pain, and their needs. What was tricky for me was the process of tuning in to them. I had spent a lifetime ignoring and repressing them, so it was very difficult for us to communicate together. But I was determined to give my very best to the healing journey, and I made every effort to listen out for and welcome everything that was coming up. Slowly, very slowly, I would start to figure out what part of me was manifesting as I found myself sucked into her vortex of incredibly painful emotions and memories. Then we could begin our journey together.

During the Listening Prayer sessions, Lorie (the facilitator) would ask Jesus questions (all the while seeking inspiration from God), and I would listen or watch for the answers. Meanwhile, Eden would scribe it all and prayerfully cover our time together, adding her own insights and encouragement at the end. The imagery was all mine, played out in my own head and then shared with them as it came to me. Most of the time, I was an onlooker in the encounter, but occasionally I got to participate when my adult Fi input was needed.

Over time my attitude toward my inner children changed, not least because I got to watch Jesus, the embodiment of real love, interacting with them. He was relentlessly kind, loving, patient, compassionate, and tender. He always treated them with respect, inviting them, never forcing them, and honouring their choices and their readiness (or not) for change. One of the most powerful contributions he made was to consistently validate their feelings and their understanding, even if it was wacky or flawed. It was heartwarming and deeply comforting that he was always on their side and determined to hang in there with them. Sometimes he was funny, and often he was ingenious. He used every which way to woo them and win their trust, without which there could not have been the exchange that he was looking for: a letting go of their pain in exchange for his gifts of freedom and hope. As I watched him caring for these wounded parts of me that I had so vehemently rejected, he was showing me a new way of caring for myself.

I had always thought that loving myself was selfish and, therefore, wrong. Besides which I really did not think there was anything in me worth loving! But the Jesus who visited my imagination challenged all that, and he began to teach me that the "Way of Love" needed to start with me. Slowly, I discovered what it was to mother my own Little Ones, to believe in them, nurture them, and tend to their needs. My own internal dialogues changed from harshness to gentleness as my heart softened and opened and as I too fell in love with all the little Fi's who resided inside me. I got to reparent and cherish them in partnership with Jesus.

There were times when everything went quiet, and I got to forget about my inner turmoil for a stretch of several months, but then it would all come surging up again, and we would return to the Kindness Room. The final leg of the journey brought with it what I called the "Big Six," the last six of my potent child parts. These largely concerned the patterns I used for communication in conflict and with people of authority. Over a six-month period, they received the healing they needed, and in June 2007, the last of the torment finally ebbed away. I waited, expecting a resurgence in the coming weeks and months, but none came. It was finished.

The stories in this book are a collection from just some of those Little Ones and their encounters during Listening Prayer. Over the three and a half years, a total of around twenty-seven child parts needed to be heard, known, and embraced. I have picked about a dozen for this book. To make them more readable, I have dropped the facilitator's questions and tried to just follow the flow of the healing encounters. Many of the prayer sessions left the stories unfinished or were just fragments. They often spanned several days, weeks, or months as the pieces for just one part of me slowly came together. It was painstaking work. Rarely did a Little One's journey have a beginning, middle, and an end. Those few that did were a real treat! And you, like me, will probably notice that the direction for each healing does not necessarily follow a logical trajectory. At one time this troubled me, but I do not think it matters anymore. It all finds its place in the bigger picture of a life in pieces coming together to form a whole and harmonized person.

You will be forgiven for thinking that this kind of healing brought nothing but clear sailing to my future! The reality was that the fallout affected one relationship in particular. In the summer of 2007, when the last of the Big Six was finally settled and at peace, I cautiously emerged from under the layers of "wounded child" and began to live for the first time as "woman." This meant I was no longer able to continue in the codependency of my marriage, a codependency that had relied on my neediness. My husband was unable to accept that I now considered myself his equal and that I had come to believe I could think for myself. The basis of our marriage functioning was the dysfunction of fundamentalist patriarchy. I remained in the home for another thirteen years in order to provide stability for my two sons as they grew up and completed their schooling, but the marriage was over.

Then in the summer of 2008, my mother died suddenly and unexpectedly. Her personality had taken on monstrous proportions throughout my childhood, and she had not been able to bond with me emotionally. It was the thing I longed for most, and her passing meant it could never happen. I was devastated. Yet, within two days of her leaving this world an extraordinary thing happened. I found myself, day and night, surrounded by the strongest sensation of her love for me. I was forty-six, and it was the first time I had ever felt it. This wrapping around—swaddling, if you like—of her intense love lasted three months. I felt so grateful that I had done the hard work of forgiving her and tending my soul in the years previous. I feel sure this is why it felt so natural to open myself to the possibility of her love reaching out to me over and over again in the years that followed.

A year or two later, I finally felt well enough that I could start to give back to others after receiving so much myself. I started to facilitate Listening Prayer for others under the covering of the local Listening Prayer community. I signed up for training with Brian and Della Headley and took every opportunity to practice. It has been one of my greatest joys to offer this service, especially when one of the client's inner children shows up. It is as if my own healed Little Ones bubble up and reach out a hand to their wounded child, offering reassurance and hope.

Occasionally, people ask me what my Little Ones are doing now. Because they are healed, most of them are integrated so completely with me that I really don't think of them anymore. But if I search my imagination, I do find a group of about ten of them, all ages and all dressed in white. They are usually in the garden playing on the lawn or chattering together under a tree. Often Jesus is with them, and they sit around him or on top of him in a giggling pile. Whenever they see me, they race over, shouting my name with arms outstretched to greet me. They absolutely adore me now that I have become their loving mother, big sister, and friend. They truly love me to infinity and beyond, as I do them! They have become my cheerleaders, and they root for me whenever I face something difficult or stressful. They utterly believe in me and are an infectious source of joy and hope that wells up inside of me when I need it. I am glad they haven't all melded into Fiona but still have some distinctive forms. Because they are healthy, we are in complete sync with each other. Gone are those tormented days when we resisted and abused each other. People talk about their inner voice, well, I'm lucky; I have inner voices! A chorus of sweet, loving, and free inner children, all singing in glorious harmony. I would not want to change them for anything.

How to Use This Book

First and foremost, I hope you will enjoy the stories in this book as well as Destiny's lovely illustrations. I hope you will be surprised and delighted by the Jesus you meet in these pages and that it will, if nothing else, cause you to ponder!

I'd like to think that some of these stories might be enjoyed by your children. Please be sure to read them for yourself first, just to make sure they will be a good fit.

Perhaps there will be stories that resonate with you. If so, here are some suggestions.

1. All of these stories provide multiple opportunities for your own inner child to piggyback into the story. They can then act as launching pads for your own listening. We are sometimes invited to "enter" the gospel stories of the Bible, and there is no reason why we can't also enter modern-day stories of encounters with God. Don't be afraid to follow the nudging of the Spirit (who is Wisdom), and let your imagination flow. Just be aware that it is important to provide a safe place for your inner child in the presence of Great Love (whatever form that

needs to be for you personally). Remain present in your adult self without necessarily participating or trying to fix things, and watch what God (or whoever represents unconditional love to you) does with your Little One.

2. If the reading of these stories stirs your own inner child, you might like to listen out for:
    - The function or role your younger self has played in trying to help you survive
    - Her or his hidden gifts or talents
    - Her or his messages (which you may or may not have pushed away)
    - What has kept her or him from freedom and growing up?
    - What has been your attitude toward your younger self until now?

3. Consider what you learn about Divine Love as you read. Has your own dear heart experienced the love that these Little Ones have witnessed? Explore the possibilities, and allow that Great Love to come close to you. Our imaginations can be a wonderful vehicle for this.

If you are someone with many wounded Little Ones or someone who supports a person like this, I hope this book will inspire hope and encouragement. The journey may be long, but it will be worth it.

THE CAVE:
AN INVITATION TO MATURITY

The cave you fear to enter holds the treasure you seek.
—Joseph Campbell

Cave, with the kind permission of David Hayward

Cave is a drawing by David Hayward, a Canadian artist, cartoonist, speaker, and writer. I first discovered it in his beautiful book, *The Liberation of Sophia* (2014), a collection of drawings and meditations of a woman named Sophia (a depiction of his soul) and her struggle to achieve independence and freedom. I have kept this book close by me for some years now because its images mirror so much of my own journey, and I have found it a great comfort. This particular picture captivated me. I completely resonated with it. I was like Sophia, standing at the entrance to the dark cave of my own heart not knowing what was inside and wondering if I dared enter and take a look.

To me this picture offers an invitation (or even a challenge!) to enter our own cave, our own dark and unknown places of troubling thoughts, trapped emotions, and untended traumas, everything within us that we have chosen to hide or forget (for whatever reason). If we do not accept the invitation, we will never be whole and healthy, and we will never fully mature. Believe me, that which is hidden in our darkest recesses will eventually catch up with us and will start to adversely affect our mental health, our behaviour, and our relationships.

Here are four questions you might like to consider. (I have answered them for myself not as I think now but as I used to think when I feared my own darkness. Your answers may be quite different.)

1. Why have I feared entering my dark places?

Embarrassment and shame mostly. I just wanted to be done with my past and my childish responses to life. Plus, why would I choose to revisit something that was so unbearably painful?

2. Why have I feared truly knowing myself?

I don't think I ever thought I was worth knowing! I figured if other people didn't really want to know me, as was my perception at the time, why would I want to know me? Also, someone had once referred to my heart as a Pandora's box, and I was afraid of what horrors might be hidden inside.

3. How can I hope to be fully loved by others if I never allow myself to be fully known?

I suppose I never dreamed I would be loved by others, and I felt certain that if they knew even half of the crazy mess inside of me, they couldn't love me anyway. While I longed to be known (because then I would know I was loved), I was so afraid of frightening others away by my internal madness. If anything, I felt that people needed to be protected from ever having to know me.

4. How can I ever say that I have learned to love and accept myself if I do not even know myself?

Loving myself was immensely difficult while I still considered my enemy to be within me. I have had a tendency to be overly critical and judgemental of others, but this was magnified a hundredfold against myself. Even when I started to discover more about my internal world, it was unhelpful until I had begun the journey of forgiving and accepting myself.

My personal discovery has been that *the more I know myself, the more I know God*. Risking getting closer to myself has been an unexpected gateway to getting closer to him. My faith journey had reached a point of stagnation. Daring to enter my own cave became the catalyst that propelled me into an entirely new and extraordinary dimension of spiritual life. The more I have embraced all that is hidden in my dark, secret self, the more I have discovered the light and the goodness of the Creator within me. It turns out he was waiting for me in the cave! Who knew? It is a precious mystery.

When you look at David Hayward's picture, and you imagine the cave as a place inside of you, what do you think might be hidden in there?

Here is a list that might get you started: depression, mental illness, sexuality, addictions, fears, past hurts and traumas, failings, things we are unable to forgive, parts of ourselves we despise or are ashamed of, deep losses, all our triggers and soapboxes.

For me, what was hidden in my cave had become my enemy. This secret internal stuff limited me, tripped me up, stopped me being who I wanted to be, and popped up uninvited at such inconvenient moments, embarrassing and humiliating me in front of others! My response was frustration and anger toward myself. I don't know when it happened, but I came to loathe, hate, and despise my inner self.

Jesus has a very simple solution for dealing with our enemy. Namely, love. Learning to love ourselves can be the epitome of loving our enemy. I hardly know of anything harder.

Therefore, should we ever decide to enter our cave, we need to make a decision to be clothed only in love. We cannot go in there to drive out the darkness—guns blazing, tongues lashing, fingers pointing. Remember, the cave usually holds pain, trauma, and shame. To enter, it is very important that we first lay down our self-accusations, our need for control, our desire to deny or minimize the pain, our self-pity, our "Why don't you just grow up?," and our "I can fix this!"

Our caves contain that within us that feels inaccessible and untouchable, parts of ourselves that we cannot change. Not even through prayers and tears or monumental human effort.

I have another mystery for you: *Love is the key to transformation*. Always. Love changes us. I cannot explain it, but those out-of-reach parts of me that God and I have embraced and loved are becoming healed and are becoming a gift to me, even the ugliest and vilest of them. They are becoming a source of inner wisdom.

What's more, I have been thrilled to discover that *the more we are transformed by love, the more we become ourselves*. The more I give God's love freedom in my cave, the less of my junk there is, and the more of the real Fi I discover. Finding out who I am and what my gifts and strengths are has been such a surprising joy! Internally, I am like the cosmos, ever growing and expanding! Letting God teach me how to love myself has not shrunk me; rather, it has enlarged me and made me better at loving others. It turns out the treasure hidden in my cave was me! Just as the treasure hidden in your cave is you!

I have visited my cave for fifteen years now. It is no longer such a scary place for me. For example, these last couple of months, I have struggled with anxiety and fear to some degree every day. But now I know to go into my cave (where I hide these emotions) with compassion and wrap my arms around my fearful self, to let her rest her head on my shoulder and to hold her shaking hand. I don't tell her she can do better, I don't beat her over the head with scriptures, I don't rebuke her for her lack of faith and trust, and I don't pretend she's not there and stuff her down into the darkness. Instead, I look her in the eye and say, "We're going to get through this together, Sweet Fi. God will give us wisdom and courage for all that is ahead." I have spread my nets out among my trusted friends and asked for opportunities for my fearful self to have her voice heard and validated over cups of tea and walks through the woods. They too will be with me through all that is coming. This way even my darkness is held by God, my community, and me.

And to you, dear friends, I wish you courage on your journey. Should you ever find yourself looking into the dark abyss of your own heart and wondering if you dare proceed, I say, "Do not be afraid!" The light and goodness of the Creator awaits you inside. Strip off your garments of self-accusation and shame. Clothe yourself in love and compassion, and tiptoe in gently and humbly. You will be led. He will light your path. And you, just like Jesus of Nazareth, will experience the transforming power and wonder of life-giving Resurrection Love in the cave. It is extraordinary, but we too can rise like a phoenix from the ashes of our past.

INTO THE SILENCE

I linger in the doorway
reluctant to step over the threshold
he stands before me
his hand held out in invitation
"Come, Dear One, I'll show you the way"
I take his hand, and he leads me into the unknown
into the silence, into the darkness
deeper into the emptiness

my heart pounds
I am afraid
can this be right?
I thought being a God-follower meant being led
into light and joy and freedom
"Trust me," he whispers

we stop for a moment, a pause on our descent
he takes my hands and looks into my face
it is not necessary to speak; his eyes say it all
"It's going to be alright Fi"
he breathes, I breathe
he waits till calm comes

then we walk on, hand in hand
into the sorrow, into the heartache
ever deeper into the desolation

something is drawing me, tugging me forwards
it's not just the hand that I grip so tightly
it's also the sound
the cry of those forgotten
the desperate call of those buried alive
huge walls appear before me
great grey stones piled as high as the eye can see
I sense there are "beings," barely still human,
trapped behind the rocks
totally isolated, completely alone
I give him a questioning look
and his face tells me I'm intuiting right
yet, this I know
this place is somewhere in his heart, for his heart
has room in it for all
there's not a soul that he would abandon to its fate
instead, he endures with them through their
desolation
each and every one has a place in him
here are the voiceless ones
chained to walls and radiators
prisoners
slaves
abused
festering
interminable pain
unbearable living
. . . but not forgotten, at least not by him

we drop to our knees

hearts pulsing with waves of grief
throats too tight to make a sound
a silent lament oozing from every pore
I lose myself in his emotion
we are one for that moment
resonating in harmony with the crushed and the broken

now we are alone again
just him and me
our faces wet with tears
I rest my head against his shoulder, and he rests his head on my head
we just breathe; that is all
we wait

he stands and offers me his hand again
I take it, and he leads me on
deeper into the silence, deeper into the darkness
deeper into the emptiness

as we walk, I notice that my life is slipping away
I become less and less able to find words to think and speak
muteness creeps into my voice box
musical notes dance their way out of my heart, and they do not return
even the words of other people become harder and harder to recognize
I see their lips moving, but I can no longer make sense of what they are saying
now I am scared
this volume of quiet is unnerving me
I feel trapped and isolated in an alien world

a world without words
but if I have no words, if I can no longer speak
how can I express my thoughts, my worship,
and my prayers?
who am I without speech?
I wrestle with the discomfort
I resist my helplessness
and I console myself
at least I still have love in my heart
that counts for something, doesn't it, Jesus?
at least I can still love and care for others through actions
that is surely enough isn't it, Jesus?

he gives me this little smile
the tender smile of one who knows how
desperately I need to love
and who also knows what is going to happen next

the darkness surrounds us
it seeps into our bones
it chills and squeezes our lungs
the world I once knew feels far, far away now
I don't like this journey
I wish Jesus had chosen the still waters and green pastures for my walk with him
I seem to be disintegrating
a stripping down of layer upon layer
my securities and comforts are no longer within reach; they have all slipped away
it's just me and him and the dark emptiness
we walk on
one step at a time
one moment at a time

deeper, ever deeper, into the silence

and then the awful day comes when I realize that
even love has deserted my soul
its last dregs have trickled away
the rivers have dried up
the streams have evaporated
just dust and rocks left
it is so dry I can barely swallow

I panic
for now I know I am truly lost
this hand in mine cannot belong to Jesus
I must have made a mistake, for he would never
lead me this way
I rage at myself for being fool enough to enter
this journey
I should have known there is no emptiness or
darkness in his heart
this place where I find myself is not a God place;
it can't be
I must have taken a wrong turn, and now I am lost

the stranger beside me stands quietly
he does not speak
he just waits for my ranting to subside and the
gloom to set in
then he gently presses my hand to remind me he is
still with me
I search out his eyes to try and discover who he is
I am puzzled, confused
it looks like Jesus
still those compassionate eyes
still the same quiet assurance and confidence

is this really you, Jesus?
is it you who has brought me to this place
where I can no longer give or receive words
and where even the love in my heart has
disappeared?
what is left, Lord, if I cannot love?
if I cannot respond to another person's love?
I am just a lame body and a bankrupt soul
impotent
derelict
as good as dead
and how can I allow others to love me when this
is all that I am?

the silence is like the endless whiteness of the
Arctic
it is so empty and so still; not even the wind blows

yet, I glimpse something far away, way over there
I shuffle across the ice to take a closer look
surely this is not a child?
alone in this vast and hostile landscape?
is this even possible?

we approach her
her face is erased; it almost looks like a
swarm of bees
as if all the lines of her features have been
chopped up
into a thousand tiny moving pieces
her feet are trapped in a huge block of concrete
on which I see the faint imprint of the word
REJECTION
she is hopelessly imprisoned

yet Jesus seems unperturbed
or rather, he is not fazed by her appearance
he only sees a child in need; that is all

he takes a seat on her cement block and gently lays
his head against her form
I rebuke him
how can you use a child like this as a
resting place, Jesus?
she has no words, no gifts, no love
she has nothing for you
she has been like this for so long, Jesus
don't you know she may *never* change?
don't you know this may be all she will ever be?
don't you get it, Jesus? I may never change
this may be all I will ever be
I shudder at the thought
but I know that though I fear it, it is true
so horribly true
who I am now may be who I will always be

precious, precious
of infinite worth
just as she is
just as I am
yes, just as she is
and just as I am
his resting place
that place where he lays his head
to come alongside and to rest a while
where he lingers to catch his breath
and to simply "be" in the presence of the one
he loves

crikey, Lord, you turn my world upside down
you invite me to sit with my broken pieces,
my little Fi's, even my Gollums
and you ask me to rest my head against them
to linger in their presence
you ask me to lay down my strivings for transformation
to accept, without a single demand, all my emptiness and darkness
to love my unloveliness
to value and learn from my places of
deepest silence
you show me that our journey
has not only been a voyage into the recesses of my own heart
but it has also been a journey into your heart

I have heard it said that you are the Word
the Living Word
the Word Revealed
yet I once read that even heaven has need of a half hour of silence
could it be that you are not just the Word
but also the Silence?

Part 2
THE LITTLE ONES

Hidden One

One of my favourite encounters was with Hidden One. Meeting her and healing her had a profound influence on my adult life. I suspect that many of us feel that our truest self is hidden within us, too afraid to be seen or known. The fact that mine made herself known to me as a vulnerable young child helped me to feel some measure of tenderness toward her, and this undoubtedly aided her healing.

At that time I had been struggling with powerful self-hatred, and I was weighed down with a loathing for what I believed was my "stinking, dirty, rotten, cowardly" heart. Sadly, this was not an uncommon reality for me. Cycles of self-criticism had dogged me for as long as I could remember.

* * *

Jesus and I are in the Kindness Room when in walks Hidden One, just a little girl, perhaps three or four years of age. She has brought her teddy bear with her and clutches him to her chest. The bear is well worn and a little bit grubby around his frayed edges, no doubt from being carried wherever she goes. I sense her apprehension on entering the room. She has been summoned, and she is clearly afraid. There is nothing of any great significance to notice about her, a plain little creature, devoid of personality yet seemingly stoic. There is nothing playful about her either, nothing fun or childlike. It is quickly obvious to me that what I see before me is just her external façade, her protective shell, and I find myself hoping there is still a flicker of youthful life tucked somewhere safe inside her.

I search out her heart, nestled in the recesses of her chest, only to discover there is nothing to see but tall, grey, impenetrable walls. Her heart is a fortress! Or a prison. It is plain to see that no one can ever climb those walls. No one will ever break through, and no one will be able to reach inside. She who is hidden within is inaccessible and has become an untouchable. Oh, how sad this makes me! I have long been sensitive to the name "Untouchable" and its meaning in the caste system. It has deep significance for me and evokes grief whenever I become aware of places in myself that remain hopelessly and permanently cut off from kindness or help.

The walls before me give up their name easily. Perhaps they have been waiting for this day in hopes of liberation. "Self-preservation" is scrawled across them and shouted out from every stone. They have done their job, built to protect my truest self and keep her safe. Somehow, she must have determined that this was the only way to survive.

I look for a doorway in the grey rockface, anything that would give access to the person trapped inside, but there is none. I run my hands over the stones in sweeping arcs, searching for the ridges of a doorframe or the dent of a keyhole, all to no avail. I am on the outside, and she is on the inside, and it seems we can never meet. We might as well just pack up and go home, Jesus. Nothing can be done.

He is sitting beside me on the couch, watching my

Little One and listening to my despondent bleating. It is just as well he is never sucked into my pessimism! With a chuckle he opens his hand to show me that he already has a key! It is one of those ancient keys that might have once unlocked a secret garden on the grounds of an old stately house in my homeland. It is made of a silver metal and has beautiful intricate swirls on the end of the shaft. I am touched that something so lovely should be fitting for this part of me. Suddenly, I know the name of the key: "Unconditional Love."

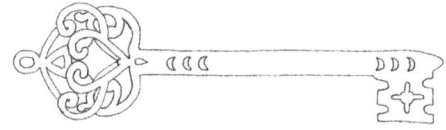

He crouches down in front of the little girl, his face so soft toward her and her little heart so hard toward him. He looks at her, and I know he sees *all* of who she is. He sees right into her hiddenness, and he loves her.

"Little One, if you would give me your walls, my love could reach you. You could make your home in my love, and my love would keep you safe."

The child does not speak. She is not used to being spoken to, nor is she used to being this vulnerable, but I can tell she is weighing Jesus's suggestion. Her eyes dart about, anxious and afraid. To be seen. To be known. To be loved. Ah, yes, she has longed for that, but can she trust him? Will she trust him?

It feels like we wait for many breaths. Finally, she seems to have made her decision. She bravely thrusts her teddy bear into his arms and in so doing allows her heart to be exposed. And there, no longer hidden, is the faint outline of a door, grey like the colour of her walls and perfectly camouflaged. Jesus lifts the key and carefully eases it into the lock. He slowly turns the key. It is a relief to me that it does not seem to hurt her.

Then he pauses. The door is unlocked, but he does not open it, not yet. Instead his eyes turn to me.

I am watching this whole scene from the sofa, and in this moment I am struck with an awful dread. I know this little girl is me as a child, who learned so young to put up sturdy walls around her heart to keep herself safe. Now that a door has been found, and a key has unlocked it, I am filled with sick apprehension at what we will discover behind that door, for I know I have a stinking, dirty, rotten, cowardly heart, and I really don't want anyone else to see it. Everything inside of me cringes.

Jesus is still looking at me, awaiting my permission. He will not open the door unless I give my consent. I hesitate, my heart thumping.

"Be brave like your Little One," he encourages me with a reassuring smile.

I hold my breath and nod, bracing myself for the worst.

Finally, the door swings open.

I sense straight away that there is so much stacked up behind that door—a backlog of what I imagine to be something putrid and revolting. But to my amazement what comes flooding out looks like a gushing waterfall of gold dust. It simply tumbles out of that little girl's heart, streaming down her chest to the floor as if released from a pent-up dam. She watches, her eyes wide. Fear turns to fascination, then delight, as it spills out and forms piles and trails. She kicks it with her little feet and its golden clouds float down softly around her. She lifts it in her hands and lets it fall through her tiny fingers. She squats down and draws patterns in it. It is making her smile! Whichever way she moves it just keeps on falling out of her gaping heart! Gold dust everywhere! There is such palpable joy in the room. Jesus is smiling too, for he knew all along what treasure was hidden inside her.

I realize as I watch her that the gold dust is love. It is all the love that I have stored up in my heart from when I was small, love that I have been too afraid to show to others for fear of rejection and for fear of all the bad names it would be called.

After a while Jesus turns to me and asks if I will accept this child, this part of me who has seemed so unreachable until now. "Yes!" I reply immediately, for I love her already, I can't help myself! I open my arms to her, and she climbs right into my heart with a great big smile on her sweet, shy face and laughter in her eyes. And there I now sit, with gold dust tumbling out of *my* chest! It falls on the couch and the floor around me. Wherever I go and whatever I do, it won't stop leaving a trail.

Letting love fall softly around me. Leaving love behind me when I move through life. Learning to love without fear or guilt. An open heart, a brave heart. Finally, I know and accept my essence. I am Fi who loves to love! Always have, always will. It is what I was made for, and it is my truest self.

The Unaffirmed Ones

I had been working on my Listening Prayer healing journey for eighteen months and had learned that discovering more hidden parts of myself could come about by many different means. The imagination is a creative engine, and it used anything it could to awaken me to lost and suppressed inner messages that were seeking to be heard.

* * *

Today, the image of a cavity in my tooth has been playing on my mind. I don't have a cavity, but the mental picture keeps coming to me and wants to draw me in. So, I follow it and wonder where it will lead. The opening to this cavity is small, but once I enter, the hole in my tooth is actually a large cavern. Could this be the home of more of my inner children?

It appears that a group of street children inhabit this empty space. They live in the semi darkness without comfort or warmth, barefoot and dressed in rags. They are older children, and some are even teenagers. I notice they are half starved and that they fight each other for any scraps they can find.

It comes to me that the food they are waiting for is "Affirmation." Occasionally, scraps of delicious affirming words are tossed in through the small opening. They fall to the bottom of that great cavern, making a tinny, tinkling sound as they hit the ground. The girls come running from the dark hiding places in a frenzy to devour these miserly crumbs.

It is an ugly picture. There is a selfishness about these children, survival of the fittest, grabbing, snatching, stealing, taking. They are driven by such a terrible hunger gnawing in their bellies. Preserving self is their highest priority, and they do not care about the needs of others. How can they when they are so deprived themselves?

I invite Jesus to this dark place.

I see him dropping a long rope down from the opening of the cavern. He climbs down the rope wearing a backpack and sets up camp on the cave floor. Within a short time, he has made a campfire, and he sleeps on the ground next to it at night.

The girls have all faded into the shadows, to the cold, dark places where they cannot be seen. They watch, silent and afraid, so still they can barely breathe. He knows they are there, but he does not look for them or even glance into the darkness. He appears absorbed in his fire and his camp, and I have the impression he is setting up for a long stay. This is going to take some time. There is no magic wand that will transform this space or heal the hearts of these suffering children. I watch and I wait to see what will happen.

I notice that the entrance to the cavern has been closed. No light comes in anymore, for a large stone has been rolled over it. Now the only light comes from Jesus's campfire. Flickering orange and yellow flames with hints of transparent blue shoot faltering light into the darkness.

Closing the opening means that no more scraps of affirmation can be thrown in, so now there is no food for these children. All there will be is Jesus's words, should he choose to speak. The eyes of every child are upon him. He has become the sole focus of their attention, with his warm glowing fire in this otherwise empty, dank place.

Maybe it is the next day, maybe it is a few days later, but I see him preparing food for himself on the fire. It could be bacon and eggs; it smells so good! Even my mouth waters!

There is movement and whispering in the shadows. One of the older girls, a teenager, has been elected as spokesperson. She steps out from the darkness and begins to approach Jesus. Scrawny, emaciated, and sick looking yet also strong somehow. She is a survivor, after all.

"Sir, we are desperately hungry. Could you give us something to eat?"

Jesus looks up from his cooking and studies her face. "How many of you are there?"

"Sir, we are many, but just a little food will be enough."

He seems to think for a moment. "I will feed you," he replies. "Tell your friends to come and sit around my fire, and I will give you something nourishing."

After a few moments, they start to appear in the half-light where the light is farthest from the fire, and the darkness begins. Their forms are visible though not distinct. They sit cross-legged in a double circle, each facing the light, a couple dozen of them.

Jesus reaches into his backpack and pulls out some tin cups. He has a big pot warming on the fire. It contains thin milk sweetened with a little honey, and he ladles some into each cup before giving them to the girl who had spoken to him. As she passes the cups to the other children, I sense the hard choice made by each child as they hand the cups to their neighbours. Not one child sips until each child is holding her own cup. I can see the intensity of the longing to drink in each child's face and the struggle to wait.

Finally, as the spokes-girl lifts her cup to her mouth, the other children follow suit. I can hear the involuntary sighs of satisfaction as the warm, sweetened milk passes over their lips. They sip silently, savouring each tiny drop, totally absorbed in this moment of unspeakable pleasure.

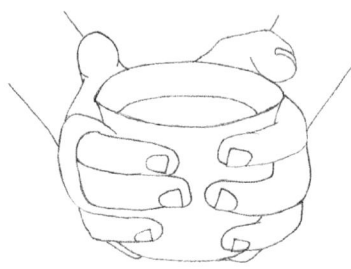

Jesus speaks quietly, though he could have been talking to himself, for none of them are listening, so focused on the goodness in their hands.

"These cups contain my words of promise for your future. Drink, Little Ones, to a brighter tomorrow, for you will yet live in a land of plenty, flowing with milk and honey. A spacious place, a safe place, a fruitful place."

After some minutes they have finished drinking, but none of them move. This feels like holy ground, one of those sacred moments when one should be still and silent.

Time passes.

"What are your names?" Jesus finally asks the spokes-girl.

She says she has never thought of it. She doesn't think they have any names.

"Well, I'm going to call you the 'Go-Getters,'" Jesus

says with a smile.

This brings a murmur of response from the children. They exchange glances and share nods of agreement. I think they like the name.

"And what should we call you, sir?"

"Just call me Jesus."

"Will you be staying a while?"

"Yes, I'll be here a while. I will not be leaving without you."

Over the next few days, I see the girls sleeping in the half-light at the edge of the darkness. No longer do they disappear into the dark places. Jesus continues to feed them the thin milk and honey. They don't seem to quarrel or fight anymore, and a peace and harmony are developing among them as there is now sufficient food for everyone. They are no longer famished and driven to insanity with hunger. They still look far too thin, but their stomachs are satisfied, and they have energy for more than just survival. I can tell they are feeling more comfortable around Jesus. He is still relating to them through the one girl, but it is becoming obvious that they like his light much more than the darkness they used to live in, and they are gradually gravitating closer to him, like moths to a bright light. There is a feeling of safety and home when they are near him.

Jesus no longer refers to them as just *the* Go-Getters. Now I've overheard him speaking of them as *my* Go-Getters. He is becoming their friend and their hope.

There is a growing sense of well-being among the girls, a distinct feeling that they are somebodies and no longer nobodies. They are starting to take on an identity, an uprightness, a feeling of worth and value, and they are beginning to recognize this in each other.

They seem pleased that Jesus is making a claim on

their lives. The fact that he now calls them my Go-Getters means he has an attachment to them. They have never had an attachment to a grown-up before. He is becoming their mentor and hero, and what is more, his name for them attributes purpose. Could there be more to life than this miserly prison? Could there be more to reach for than just crumbs of affirmation? Jesus is nourishing more than their bodies; he is feeding their souls.

It is a week or two later. Today I am only seeing the one girl, the spokes-girl; the others are gone. The many parts have harmonized, joined together into the one, though the imagery still takes place in the underground cavern, in a wholly dark place.

I see Jesus sleeping on the ground by the campfire, and I see the child, a young woman really, lying at his feet under his blanket. She is waiting for him to awaken and discover her there. She slipped under his covers while he was asleep, for she has decided to give her life to him. It was he, after all, who came to rescue her and gave her hope when there was only darkness, hunger, and monotony. It is to him that she has chosen to belong.

When I see her again, she is a young woman in her twenties. I had expected the scene to shift from the dark cavern underground, but Jesus is still there with her. He seems to want to keep her fully dependent on him for just a bit longer, until she is stronger. He is imprinting his reassurance in her, and something solid and dependable is maturing within her. I do not hear what he says to her, but I sense that he is feeding her a steady diet of healthy, healing words, and I see a deep trust and affection developing between them.

I sense that Jesus is preparing this woman to stand in the world. And when that time comes, I can picture that she is going to be a like a tall white pillar, secure and strong. No longer will she need reassurance from others to know that she exists and to know who she is, Jesus will have already planted that within her. When I study the stonework of this elegant pillar, I see that it is intricately inscribed with many beautiful words and symbols. Jesus has taken the time, as a master stonemason, to make these lasting inscriptions on her heart in the cavern so that one day she will be ready for real life.

Fetus Fi

In my imagination I had been seeing a woman lying in darkness in the fetal position. She was a follow-on from the Unaffirmed Ones who had become the Go-Getters. The girl remaining with Jesus in the cavern had asked when they might leave the dark space, and Jesus had replied that there was one more thing that needed to happen before they could go. It was on the back of this that I started to see the woman in the fetal position. She led me to discover a new and complex part of myself. This new part was engulfed in shame and utter wretchedness. She felt far, far away and had the sensation of being in outer space. She was distant from life, inaccessible, and did not have the strength to re-enter Earth's atmosphere.

At some point I met her in a dream. This was unusual for me, but it expresses how potent she was and how deeply she was clamouring to reach me from my subconscious. In the dream she slid into a kind of hellhole. It was an eerie, frightening place without light, yet the walls were glowing red with blood. She was alive but like a dead thing. These words came to me from her: "Always dying yet never dead, always living yet never alive." I was afraid for her; her existence was an endless purgatory. It was gruesome, for she was being eaten alive by wild animals and demons. I could hear their roaring and the sounds of them devouring her like lions or hyenas at a kill. Her body was being ripped apart and strewn about. In my terror I was trying to grab hold of the hands of my Listening Prayer counselors, clutching at anyone who would reach out to me, trying to keep connected with the world above and not get lost forever in that terrible place.

For some reason I could not seem to find Jesus there. Except perhaps for a moment when I saw his feet standing at the edge, red with blood.

At my next opportunity, I transferred this bloody scene to the Kindness Room, my safe place. It finally made sense why Jesus had insisted the walls of that room be red. It was in anticipation of this day, when the bloody walls surrounding Fetus Fi would need to come for care and healing. It dawned on me that the Kindness Room was actually the Womb of God and had been all along! This Womb of Great Love had become the place of my healing, not just for the traumas sustained in my mother's womb but also for all my childhood wounding. At this tumultuous time, this revelation offered me comfort. To be nestled and cared for in the nurturing, feminine, incubating spaces of the Divine felt deeply touching.

* * *

The scene is utter carnage. Dismembered body parts, flesh, blood, and snapped and ground-up bones are splattered throughout the room, which is somehow vacated of all furniture. It looks like a horror movie set, but, thankfully, all the wild animals and demons of my dream are gone. They do not get to accompany us to the safehouse.

Jesus is there. I watch as he moves slowly around the room, and I wonder what he is doing. It becomes apparent that he is looking for something on the floor. His body is stooped over, and he is moving with unhurried intent as his eyes scan the ground. Finally, he finds what he is looking for, and he bends down to pick something up out of the bloody mess: a tiny piece of flesh, no bigger than a dime. It occurs to me that this is the only thing left that is still alive. A fragment, a remnant, she is all that remains after the massacre. He holds this shred of torn flesh ever so gently in his warm hands. There is so much emotion in his face, a look in his eyes that I cannot describe, but I know this morsel of living tissue is precious to him. He walks over to the fireplace and sits on the hearth. Sometimes he stretches out his hands to look at her. Sometimes he holds her against his chest, cupped tenderly in his palms. He is deep in thought. Perhaps he is dreaming; perhaps he is praying for this little Fetus Fi. Finally, he pops her into his breast pocket, that place closest to his heart, his marsupial pouch, to keep her safe and warm.

A week later I see Jesus again. This time he is wearing a white doctor's coat. He has been carrying my fetus part in his pocket all this time. He invites me into his doctor's office and pulls out a chair for me to sit by him. "I've got something for you," he says.

"Thank you for looking after it for me," I reply. "I honestly don't think I'd know how to take care of it myself. I feel it might get terribly neglected if it has to come back into my care."

"But, Fi, it is a part of you that you cannot do without. And 'it' is a 'she'! You need her!"

"But I don't know how to look after her," I protest, "and she's so tiny and fragile I'm afraid I might damage her, or she might shrivel up and die. It's not that I don't want to . . ."

"I know, Fi. This Little One doesn't have much of a

recognizable form, which makes it harder to love and care for her, doesn't it? Yet, within this tiny scrap are treasures and gifts awaiting to be nurtured and grown. In this fragment are building blocks and keys that will greatly affect your future life." I know what he is saying is true, so I accept her back, though I still wonder if I will ever learn to love her.

Some three months later, I get to spend a bit more time with Fetus Fi. Jesus has invited us to the Kindness Room, the red Womb Room. He and I are sitting cross-legged facing each other. My little fetus scrap is in his hands, which he is holding out in front of him.

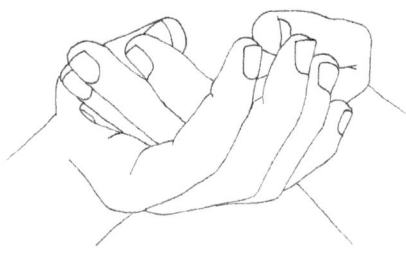

This tiny part of me cannot speak, but she still has emotions, and I can tell she is feeling desperate. Though she is wordless, the sense I get from her is, "I'm never going to make it!" She can't understand why no one wants her. The big people don't want her. They may or may not let her live. They see no value in her. She is afraid to live, afraid of what that will look like, afraid that she won't be welcomed or loved. At the same time, she is afraid to die, traumatized by the prospect that she may soon be annihilated. She has heard the sounds of her parents arguing and the sound of her father crying. She knows her very existence has caused this.

I feel great anguish on her behalf. She is so alone and pressed in on every side by all that wants to crush her. Big, muscular angels appear. They have come to make space for her to breathe, to exist. With huge effort they travail to push back the dark forces that are engulfing her. Into the new space they create around her, Trinity floods, released like powerful, pent-up tsunami waters that have been straining for years to encircle, protect, and carry this tiny mortal. Trinity envelops her—beneath her, above her, and all around her until she is fully enfolded and held in Great Love.

Some words from Psalm 23 run through my head: "Surely goodness and mercy shall follow me all the days of my life, and I will dwell in the house of the Lord forever." This is such a beautiful promise for my fragile beginning self.

* * *

My Fetus Fi had a long journey over the years of Listening Prayer. She presented at intervals as a powerful emotional soup that swirled through me and overtook me. Often, her feelings of alienation and her sense of being unwanted wearied me. She craved and clutched at connection to someone, anyone, to grasp her hand and keep her from falling deeper into the deathly abyss. She struggled to know if she existed. It sounds odd, I know, but she didn't know if she was real, if she was a person, if she really "was."

Sometimes a big, dark mama angel came and enfolded her in her enormous arms and hid her in her soft bosom. She sang a lament over her in her angel tongue.

Finally, almost a year from when I first encountered Fetus Fi, we had a breakthrough. It was an agonizing Listening Prayer session, perhaps the most difficult of our three and a half years, and it took great courage for me to remain present in it. Everything my fetus part felt, I felt. It was mind bending and body wracking. I felt like I was going mad. The scene in my imagination grew darker and darker, and I was in great panic and terror. Jesus took me in a small rowboat on a journey toward the darkness. He headed us straight into those ominous hurricane clouds, into the very heart of the fierce and deadly storm. We could not see where we were going; the sea was so rough, the waves so high, and the sky so black. Yet, he seemed to know the correct direction, and he kept pointing the flimsy boat deeper into the fury. My little part and I cried all the way, but in the end, in the very eye of the storm, he rescued and saved that which had been held prisoner for so long. I don't know how he did it. I don't even know what exactly happened, but when I arrived, shaking and exhausted, on the other side, I knew that something significant had changed. My fetus part had found peace. The torment she had endured for forty-five years was over, done, finished. No more purgatory. No more being suspended between life and death. And from that day forward, she never showed up in distress again.

Can a Statue Cry?

not even the dead left now in that lonely valley
the killing fields stripped of their booty
nothing left for the vultures to consume
untouched for forty years, the skeletons lie where
they fell
ragged cloth blowing in the breeze

he says this is part of his garden
and the day has come for him to gather in the lilies
to bring them home
but who would venture into such a haunt?
who would dare tread where so many have
been slaughtered?

the dead Christ's body still visible in the dirt
his neck snapped and bent awkwardly backwards
flesh gone but bones still in place
a testament to the truth
"what you have done to one of the least of these
you have done to me"

will the birds ever sing here again?

the gardener walks south
out of the great entrance to the graveyard
his arms laden with wreaths of lilies
symbols of death and life at one and the same time
his eyes burning with orange fire

so this is all that remains
this is the remnant
the corner torn from the mantle

can a nation be built from a remnant?
can a person be formed from a fragment?
can anything whole come from something so
incomplete,
so fractured?

and what use is a bunch of lilies anyway?
is their sole purpose to sit in a vase?

the child sits in the refrigerated truck
that place assigned to her
she leans over to the man-sized statue of Jesus
rests her head against his stony cold leg and
whispers
"Even if you never speak to me
if you never smile
if you never grow warm beside me
if you are always this man of cold cement
I will always love you
and my heart will always thank you for
searching me out
in the valley of death"

can a statue cry?

this one has two tears
that didn't make it half way down his cheeks before
they froze solid

("Fiona" means "white" or "lily")
June 15, 2006

I wrote this poem the day after that final Fetus Fi experience. It was the best I could do to capture something of the sensations of that extraordinary Listening Prayer session. You will notice that before it is even finished, the next child part is starting to make herself known. No sooner was one taken care of than the next one popped up to the surface, begging for attention and help, trying to access my thinking with her desperate needs and messages. And so, the journey continued . . .

The Bruised One

I knew that one day I would meet the Bruised One, and I had been dreading it. I suppose I was afraid of having to visit old memories and reliving the trauma. But in the event, none of that was necessary for her healing. Hers was a presence that had lived on the edge of my mind for as long as I could remember, so when I finally met her in the mansion, I was surprised to discover that she was, in fact, a multitude! She looked like a whole tribe of children, spilling into the hallway from the bedrooms upstairs and all the way down the great staircase to the front entrance. Dozens and dozens of them, dozens and dozens of us. The bigger ones were carrying the littlest ones, hanging over the banisters to peer at me as I tried to take in the scene. They looked like regular girls except for their skin, which was covered in black, blue, and green bruises, and their eyes all shared the same haunted look of suffering.

* * *

Jesus has already prepared the Kindness Room for our meeting. A cozy fire is burning in the hearth, and candles are glowing on the mantlepiece. He tells me this is a safe place and not to be afraid despite the great number of child parts affected. I start to wonder how all these children will fit in the room, but it seems that one child has been elected to represent the group, so it is only she who accompanies us. She is probably about eight years old, and when she comes closer, though she makes no sound, I see that tears are running down her cheeks. She stands obediently by the fire, its flickering light making her face shiny from the wetness.

"What is your name?" Jesus asks, breaking the silence.

"I am Bruised One."

As with many of my Little Fi's in these encounters, I discover that I know her thoughts, so even when she is not talking, I hear her inner commentary. The bruising under her skin comes from physical punishments that she believes she deserves, and she thinks she has been summoned here by this "Jesus" for more. She does not know what she has done wrong, but neither she does expect to know. She has learned that she is simply bad and that she always has been. Apparently, that means she does, says, and thinks bad things without even knowing what they are. She stands quietly, tensely, ready. She knows not to make eye contact, not to let her punisher see into her heart or her mind. It is the only form of protection she can apply. So, she keeps her eyes downcast and braces herself for whatever might happen next.

"I am *not* going to hit you," Jesus says.

After a moment, he moves forward and kneels in front of her, up close, so she cannot avoid him. He looks into her face, and says it again, very firmly. "I will *never* hit you, not ever. I am your healer and your friend, and I could never bear to hurt you."

I can tell she is puzzled, surprised, even confused, but she is listening.

"Why would you want to heal me? Why would you

want to be my friend?"

"Because I love you, Child. I will never hurt you, never. I want to carry all your pain, all your bruises inside and out. Will you let me? You have borne them long enough. Please let me take them for you."

She is at a loss, bewildered by his strange words. Nothing could have prepared her for this, but he presses on.

"Can I lay my hand over your heart, so you can feel me? If you feel my hand, you will know that I am telling the truth."

Time stands still in the Kindness Room. This sweet child wavering both mentally and physically as she stares down at the grown man kneeling before her.

My brave little girl nods quietly. She will allow him; she has nothing to lose.

He gently rests his hand against her chest, his kind eyes gazing into hers. "Can you feel it now, Little One?"

She nods again, her eyes growing bigger. She is wondering who he is and what this strange power is that she feels from his hand. It is a reassuring feeling, like warm liquid silk under his fingers, seeping into her skin, sinking into her being, and she finds herself unable to doubt him. He really does want to take away her bruises! Can this really be happening? A delicious sensation creeps through her body, a wonderful feeling of anticipation of something good and lovely.

From behind him Jesus pulls out a large transparent glass bowl and holds it out to the child. It is hand-blown and beaded with tiny air bubbles and wisps of blue, delicately made and not at all heavy.

"Here, Little One, this is for all the tears you've cried over the years. I have seen all your tears; not a moment of your life has passed by my attention. Will you put your tears in my bowl?"

Curiously, cautiously, the child reaches into her heart and carefully lifts out a large white jug. It is quite full and very heavy, but, with his help, she pours every last drop of the salty waters into his lovely bowl.

"Thank you," he says, smiling for the first time. "Each and every tear you have cried is precious and not to be wasted. This bowl of tears will be used in my garden to help the plants grow!"

She is astonished that he values her tears and that they can be used to create something beautiful. She has shed so many tears through her short life, though most of them were internal and never saw the light of day. She had no idea that her tears mattered to someone. The very thought of it touches her deeply. She has never known such kindness. She trembles a little. But he is not finished yet.

"Would you let me hold you?"

Now she is unsure, perturbed. She hesitates. "Are you safe?" she whispers.

He nods. "I promise you I am safe. I will never hurt you. They call me the Good Shepherd because I love to take care of little lambs."

He is still kneeling on the floor, and he shifts his position with his legs outstretched, so she can be held. Slowly, she climbs onto his lap and sits stiff and alert, unsure how to hold her body or where to look. But as he wraps his arms around her and gently holds her and rocks her, she starts to relax. She can feel his chest rising and falling beside her, and she can hear his breath inhaling and exhaling over her head. He strokes her hair. No one has ever done that before. It's nice! Calming. He reminds her of her beloved grandpa as he runs his fingers across her cheeks, her ears, her nose. He touches her fingernails, one at a time. She melts under his caresses until she is cuddled up against him, completely at home.

As he holds her, I realize that all the discoloration under her skin has been leaving her and going into him instead. He is literally absorbing her bruises into his body.

"I thought you made me like that," she says softly, "to be like a punching bag because I'm so bad."

Tears run down his face, and his voice breaks as he tries to reply. "No, no, Little One! I made you to be beautiful and to be a blessing. Every part of your body is made for loving, not for hating or hurting."

How astonished she is that she touches his heart so. How sad he is that she could believe such terrible things about herself. His tears drip onto her arms and legs, and they rub them into her skin together, healing her for love, not hate.

Later when she is more settled, with her permission he takes three heavy stones out of her heart. Each one represents a lie she has believed connected to her bruises. She and I are startled when he smashes those stones against the wall, but we are also strangely comforted by how passionately he wants to destroy those lies. Debris smatters the floor, and he chuckles. "Don't worry about the mess; the angels enjoy cleaning it up. They love it when they see I've been at my father's business."

Satisfied, the little girl looks around the room. Then she fixes her eyes on me, Adult Fi, sitting on the couch. Pointing at me she asks Jesus if she can come to me.

Oh, she is a dear little thing, I can't wait to spend time with her. I open my arms to her, welcoming her onto my lap. She climbs up, and before I know it, I have embraced her right into my heart, and she has disappeared! She is no longer separate from me, no longer needing to carry all the bruises of my childhood for me and living in an excommunicated space where I don't have to feel her pain. Now these Little Fi's are free of those traumas, and we can live together as one. Reconciled. Reunited. Ready to move on from our past and finally live.

The Invisible One and the Burden Express

It was only a few months into my Listening Prayer journey when this experience happened. I was growing more confident in hearing and seeing for myself, and after the initial encounter with my prayer facilitators, I was becoming able to follow up by myself, pen and journal in hand as I wrote down what I was picturing.

Trying to be invisible was one of my coping strategies during childhood. First, I didn't want to rock the boat and upset the fragile equilibrium of my mother's frightening moods, so being invisible was sometimes helpful in the home. Second, I am a natural introvert, and public recognition, even for good things, was highly embarrassing for me. Add to that the bucket loads of shame I carried about myself, and it is no wonder I wished to blend into the crowd and not be seen.

* * *

I am surprised to see the door to the Kindness Room open and then shut all by itself. It takes a moment before I realize that a little girl has come in. She is transparent, and her form only gradually becomes visible to me in faint, hazy lines, though Jesus doesn't seem to have any trouble seeing her. She stands in front of him, a nondescript little person aged about four, her eyes fixed on the floor.

"So, here is the Invisible One," he says softly, as if to himself. "Do you like not being seen?"

She does not speak out loud during the entire interview, but through some strange telepathy, Jesus and I hear her thoughts.

"No."

"Would you like to be seen?"

"No," she replies immediately, glancing up with fear-filled eyes as if he might force her to become visible. But I know she need not fear. There is no forcing with Jesus.

"Why are you unseen?" he asks.

"It's better that way."

"And is that why you don't talk?"

"Yes."

"Has someone told you to go away and to be quiet?"

Her eyes full of shame, she nods slightly.

"But I have heard you singing."

She looks up at him in shock with something close to panic on her face, her lips falling apart and her eyes wide and questioning.

"I heard a song in your heart, and it was lovely."

I am reminded of Song of Solomon 2:14: "My dove in the clefts of the rock, in the hiding-places on the mountainside, show me your face, let me hear your voice, for your voice is sweet and your face is lovely" (NIV).

"I'm a good girl!" she says somewhat desperately as if she has been caught doing something naughty.

"I know you are," Jesus replies. "You're a very good girl, and you really do try to do what you're told, don't you?"

I notice how hard her young heart is toward Jesus. His

words are nice, but there is no way she is going to let him near her tender places. She has learned to protect herself from others because she knows too much about punishment and its unexpected application. No one can be trusted; plus, she has only just met him, so he is definitely to be kept at arm's length.

But Jesus is undeterred. "I want you to know this, Little One," he says gently but firmly with an unswerving gaze. "I will *never* tell you to go away or to shut up. Never. This is my promise to you for always and always. I want to see you, to watch you, and to watch over you. I want to hear what you have to say, all of it, nothing need be left unspoken. I promise I will always listen."

His words are like water off a duck's back. The child is unresponsive, and his words disappear from her mind as quickly as they come. They just do not compute.

Jesus decides that we should take this little girl out into the garden. Perhaps the distraction will help relax her, and the fresh air will help calm her mind. I am starting to notice more about her now as her image is becoming clearer to me. She is just a youngster with pale cheeks and short, straight golden hair. She has a sombre air about her, and she moves mechanically and without any motivation other than compliance. We each hold a hand, Jesus and me, with the child between us. I notice how limply her small hand lies in mine. She is used to being led by the hand and having no say in where she is taken. She walks with us, but she has no wish to be there.

I think this might be the first time I have come with a younger self into the gardens. It is so beautiful and peaceful out here. Immediately I sense myself dialling down and soaking up nature's goodness. All the flowerbeds and pathways are well tended, and there are old stone walls with patches of lichen, up which vines, honeysuckle, and roses are climbing. There are trellises and fountains and dovecotes and borders. I notice lots of workers tending the gardens with hoes, garden forks, and spades. Whenever we pass near one of them, they stop what they are doing and turn and smile at the child. Some just cock their hats, and some say a kind word of welcome.

"Hello, Little Missy. Nice to see you out and about."

It seems to me they have eyes only for her. I feel tiny movements in her small fingers, and her hand starts to grip mine. I sense her thoughts. "Is this what it feels like to be real? Do they think I'm a person? Why are these people glad to see me? It doesn't make any sense!"

I see we have come to our swing. It is a double one hanging from a large old tree with a wide trunk, deep boughs, and gentle curves. She sits comfortably between us, and we swing in silence on this most lovely of evenings. The sun casts a warm yellow light over the garden, and blossoms are still falling from the fruit trees around us, carpeting the lawn. To my surprise, I hear the Little One start to hum quietly to herself. I listen with bated breath, trying to make some sense of the melody and not wanting to put her off in any way. How extraordinary that this insipid child should have a tune to sing! And in our presence! A couple of minutes later, Jesus starts to hum with her. It's not a song I recognize, but he seems to know it. They do not look at each other, but I sense that their hearts have begun to find a way of harmony. It is a magical moment, a breakthrough, and I wonder if now she might begin to trust him.

A few days later I check in again to find that we are still sitting on the swing, the three of us, but now the girl is sobbing. Her face is hidden in her hands, and she is curled up in a little ball beside me. I can tell that she is racked with guilt, and her inner voice is saying, "I'm sorry, I'm sorry."

I am not expecting this. *How can a child so young feel so much guilt?* I wonder. There is nothing she could be guilty of.

That thought remains with me, unanswered.

A year passes before I see the little girl again. I am having some rough nights triggered by powerful emotions of anxiety and guilt. It is then that I remember the Invisible One, and her struggles with guilt, and I wonder how she is. I know what to do. I find a quiet moment in my day, slip into my imagination, and visit the Kindness Room where I find Jesus waiting for me on the couch. He pats the cushion beside him, inviting me to join him there.

"There is someone I'd like you to meet again," he says with a twinkle in his eye.

With that the door opens, and in bounds the Invisible One, except she is no longer transparent but very much visible and full of life. I'm stunned!

"Jesus!" she shouts as she sees him and leaps onto his lap. "Can we play again?" She is breathless, and her eyes are bright and sparkling.

Jesus hugs her for a moment. "I have a special game for us to play today," he says.

She is almost quivering with excitement.

I notice a train track on the floor at our feet. It encircles the sofa, and a good-sized toy train chugs past us, blowing off steam and tooting its whistle. It pulls several empty train cars. The little girl is enraptured, spellbound by the sight.

"What are the empty cars for?" she asks.

"That's for all the stuff we don't want anymore," Jesus says. "We load it on, and it takes it all away for us. It's called the Burden Express, and it's good at getting rid of things we don't need to keep."

"Can I put something in it, Jesus?" she asks excitedly.

"I was rather hoping you would."

"But what? I don't have anything."

"Look inside your heart."

She pauses for a moment. "Oh, I see!" She peers down at her chest, opens the door of her heart, and starts to rummage around inside.

"Can I get rid of absolutely anything?" she asks, "Anything at all?"

"Absolutely anything," Jesus replies with a grin.

"Then the first thing you can have is this. I call it my 'scolding mirror' 'cos whenever I look at myself in it, it scolds me and tells me I'm a naughty girl."

"That's a great thing to get rid of," Jesus says, smiling as she lumbers it into one of the train's wagons. "That sure has given you a hard time, hasn't it?"

"Oh, it's awfully mean to me. It often makes me cry."

Next, she pulls out a long walking stick.

"I call this my 'hitting stick,'" she says. "It's always telling me I'm going to get punished, and even though it doesn't often hit me, it's always bullying me and bossing me around. It's a really scary stick, and I hate it. Could your train take that too?"

Jesus nods.

"Yahoo!" she cries. "Goodbye, hitting stick, Jesus says I don't have to keep you!"

Then she presents her dolly.

"This is 'crybaby,'" she says, "'cos she does lots of crying for me when I'm not allowed to." She looks a bit nervous. "You see, I don't like her, Jesus, 'cos she's always sad, and she's always making that crying noise. It gets on my nerves. But the thing is," she pauses, "what will I do if I feel like crying?"

Jesus smiles. "From now on," he says quietly, "you can let your tears come out of here." He points to her eyes.

"Really?" Her eyes widen.

"You don't have to hold that crying baby in your heart anymore. You can let your tears slide out of your eyes, and I will hold you and wrap you in my arms until you feel all better."

Her expression is incredulous.

"Really!" he assures her.

There is a moment's pause as she decides whether she can believe him. "You mean you won't ever get mad at me if I cry?"

He laughs. "Never."

She almost throws the doll into the train car. "Then you can go crybaby 'cos I don't need you anymore!"

Next, she pulls out yards and yards of heavy black material. "This is my 'hiding cloak,'" she says. "It smells yucky, see?" She shoves it into Jesus's face, and he wrinkles his nose.

"It's very old," she says with a sigh. "I've had it a long time. It used to hide me ever so good when I was a baby, and no one would find me for hours. But it's kind of stuffy in there now, and I'd much rather be playing out in the garden instead. Besides, you miss me when I hide under it, don't you?" A sweet little smile plays on her lips.

"Indeed, I do, Little One."

"Help me put it in the train car, Jesus."

They heave and lug it together until the last fold is stuffed into the train car.

The train is quite full now, and the little girl claps excitedly as it puffs away behind the couch. The steaming engine continues its circuit and reappears, but now the scolding mirror, the hitting stick, the crying baby, and the hiding cloak are all gone, and the train returns to her, bearing gifts in its cars. Her clapping has turned to joyous squeals. I want to put my fingers in my ears!

The first car that had once held the scolding mirror now contains a small plaque to hang on her wall. It reads, "You are beautiful—inside and out!" It is decorated with tiny painted flowers in soft pinks, blues, and yellows. Perhaps they are forget-me-nots and buttercups; I cannot tell, but I know they are flowers of the meadow where things grow wild and free.

The second contains a long wooden shepherd's staff with a crook on its end. When it first disappeared behind the couch, that car held the hitting stick that used to threaten and abuse her.

"You are my little shepherdess," Jesus says, "and you will never hit or bully the sheep with the staff of authority. Instead, you will lead them with love and compassion."

In the third car the crying baby is no longer there. In its place is a tickling feather! Yes, a feather that tickles! This is a sneaky gift because it has a way of sneaking up on you to give you a tickle when you least expect it!

"But Jesus, I'm so ticklish. That's not fair!"

"I know," he says with a wink, "but I'll let you in on a secret: so am I!"

As the penny drops, she grabs the feather and begins to chase him around the couch. I watch this wild, irreverent scene and listen to their shrieks and giggles. They end up in a heap on the floor with Jesus pretending to beg for mercy. She has a tender heart; she stops tickling him, and they rest on their backs feeling warm and breathless.

"I have one more gift for you," he says.

"There's more?" she whispers, angling her head, so she can see his face.

Out of the last train car, the one in which they had heaped the hiding cloak, he pulls a white dress, which he holds up to her. Her mouth drops open, speechless with wonder. The dress is covered in glass beads, and as the light catches them, each one has a tiny rainbow of light in it.

"I'd love for you to wear this frock," he says. "You will look lovely in it. Whenever people see you wearing it, they will see all the colours of my love and my promises, and then they will know that there is hope."

Her eyes shine! His heart melts.

Now I see my little Fi clad in her rainbow dress of hope, her shepherdess staff in one hand, her tickling feather of joy in the other, and the plaque of beauty behind her.

I receive her back into my heart with my arms open wide, for she is laden with all the good and wonderful gifts Jesus has given her and free of the burdens that once weighed her down.

When first we met, she was invisible and silent. She didn't even know if she really existed, and she trusted no one. Now she comes to me as a joyful, healthy child, very present and very real! She integrates back into me, the adult Fi, and she enriches my life. She helps me when I'm dogged by guilty feelings and when I fall back on old coping mechanisms. She helps me let go of them, forgiving myself and opening myself to all that Love wants to give to me.

The Insignificant One

In my mind's eye, I had been seeing a group of a dozen or more children holding hands in an unbroken circle. They were of many ages, from toddlers to teenagers. Some of the older ones were carrying babies on their backs. They stood in a ring that was, I sensed, inward looking and exclusive. They believed they were the Insignificant Ones, unworthy of being remembered. They felt overlooked, ignored, forgotten, and laid aside. Each one carried much pain, but they had a strong unity together and a feeling that they understood and shared in one another's sorrows. They were locked into their abandonment, and their abandonment was locked into them. If they ever spoke of their pain, people called it self-pity, so they preferred to remain separate and alone.

I also had a sense that their ears were forever inclined toward "Mum" (though she was nowhere to be seen) just in case she might have a change of heart, reach out her arms to them, and express that they did matter to her after all.

I decided to take these "Insignificant Ones" to the Kindness Room.

* * *

They shuffle into the room in a muddle, insisting on keeping their arms firmly linked in their circle.

"Welcome, welcome," Jesus says as he rises from the sofa and opens his arms to greet them, a big smile on his face. "It's lovely to see you all. I've been so looking forward to our time together."

They glare at him silently while he waits for them to find a spot to stand in the center of the big red room. He is unperturbed by their behavior and their insistence on solidarity.

"I have been watching you in your playroom, and I see how well you take care of each other; you never leave anyone out! And you seem to invent all sorts of interesting games. What is that game I've seen you play when you walk around and sing your song?"

The children didn't know they had been watched. It feels strange to have been spied on. Their silence is broken by an older girl with a small voice. She does not expect to be understood, but she is polite. "That's our 'matter' song, sir. 'You matter, I matter, we all matter.' We sing it to each other to keep ourselves going." Her eyes are glistening, and she is struggling to hold back her emotions.

"Ah, I see." Jesus's reply is gentle, even reverent. "And how does it make you feel when you all sing that song?"

A single tear creeps down her cheek. She holds her face steady but makes no reply. He repeats his question, only this time even softer, with a tilt of his head. "And how does it make you feel, Little Ones?"

She has not taken her eyes off him. She knows she cannot lie, for she can tell he already knows the answer. "It feels like our hearts are full of broken glass, sir, and as we sing our song, it's as if we run our fingers back and forth over that glass to try and soothe it, but it only hurts us more." She bites her bottom lip.

Some of the children look nervous, exchanging furtive glances. An invisible barometer of fear and anxiety has just massively elevated. It feels incredibly uncomfortable for these children to be made known to this stranger. They would desperately like to leave, and soon.

"Peace, Little Ones," Jesus responds. "I will not harm you. I have the answer for the longings of your hearts, and if you let me, I will help you to find it.

"I am grateful to you for caring for each other and especially to you big girls for looking after the small ones and for helping to carry each other's pain. It is so good that you banded together to help each other through. You have made a difference, and I am very proud of you.

"I would love to help you carry some of that pain, to make it a little easier for your hearts. Even from here I can feel how much you are all hurting. Would you let me bear some of it for you?"

His short speech comes so unexpectedly to the children. They are taken aback. Not only does he not judge or condemn them, he actually validates them and is offering something they had not imagined possible: the chance to be free of the pain of not mattering to the person whose love they crave most.

"How would you do that, sir? We will not allow you to separate us. We belong together."

"Oh no, I would never try to break you up, I know you need each other, but if you will allow me to sit in the center of your circle, you can all sit around me and press your feet against me, and then I'll be able to start to relieve you of some of this pain. I'll take it into me!"

He waits for a moment, allowing them time to think. After all, his suggestion is rather strange!

"We don't know why you would want to help us, sir,

but we will try to do as you ask, if it really will take away some of this hurt."

Jesus waits no longer. He is on his hands and knees crawling under the linked arms of two of the bigger children and finding his place on the floor in the middle of their circle. He sits cross-legged and expectant. Slowly, they sit down too, their legs stretched out toward him, though careful not to lose their physical connection with each other.

"Our feet might not be very clean, sir."

"I don't mind a bit," he says, gently helping each child place her feet against him.

They sit for an uncomfortable minute. "Nothing seems to be happening, sir." It had been a stupid suggestion. Of course nothing was going to happen!

Jesus smiles. "It will very, very soon. But first I have to tell you who I am and why I brought you here. My name is Jesus," I hear his name being whispered around the circle, "and I have a specially shaped heart designed to carry all the broken glass from other people's hurting hearts. In my heart there is *so* much love." His hands erupt up to draw big, excited firework arcs in the air. "It's like the hottest furnace you can imagine, and all that broken glass just melts into liquid glass, which I can then use to make anything I choose. It's one of my favourite things, to take the broken things in people's hearts and make them into something new. I love it! All you have to do is say in your heart, 'Jesus, you can take all my broken bits . . .'"

Before he can say another word, a small child, about three years old, interrupts with the words, "Jesus, take all my brokey bits."

They all turn to look at her, her sad little eyes staring intently up at him.

"Thank you, Little One," he murmurs softly.

Her face starts to change, a slow smile tugging at the corners of her mouth. "Feels nice, Jesus," she whispers.

"It does, doesn't it, sweetheart?" His smile gets bigger.

I look around the circle. Some children are asking him in their hearts, and others are asking him out loud. The room's atmosphere is changing, and their faces are expressing relief from their pain with grins and tears of amazement. Even the babies on the bigger girls' backs seem more peaceful and relaxed. One is gurgling, and another has hiccups. A ripple of hushed laughter passes around the circle. Jesus joins in. He seems so happy and in his element with all these dear Little Ones pressing their feet against his legs and his back. I leave them then to talk and share stories and to dream of a new life ahead.

Some days later I visit the scene again. Jesus is still with the children, inside their circle, but he's standing now. He is walking around to each one, handing out a cup of wine and a piece of bread. "This is my blood, shed for you. This is my body, broken for you."

I watch from a little ways off. He has told me to keep back and let him do this bit. The children seem OK to take the elements. I know that Jesus wants each one of them to know that they matter to him. They matter enough that he would be willing to lay down his life if it would show them how much he loves them, but I know they don't understand this mystery yet. How can they?

When communion is finished, Jesus asks if he might join their circle. They hesitate, but after some discussion among themselves, they cautiously agree. In fact, this is the first time anyone from "outside" has been included in their circle. They look somewhat apprehensive, afraid he might impose some new rules on them or, worst of all, try and break them up.

Once he is seated between a teenager and a youngster, Jesus speaks. "Thank you for letting me be a part of your group. I feel very honoured that you have allowed me in. I have been watching you all with great interest for a long time, and I was hoping for the day when you would let me be a part of you."

Now I notice what must be that furnace fire in his heart that he spoke about last time, for his chest is glowing warmly orange through his clothes. The children are looking at it too. It's strange! He asks them if they know why it is burning so hot inside him today. Again, it is a mystery, and none of them seem to know the answer. But then that same little girl, the three-year-old, exclaims with a giggle, "It's 'cos you loves us, Jesus!"

The group reacts, shocked at her crazy suggestion that this stranger would love them. They strongly disapprove; perhaps they are even offended. She might as well have uttered an obscenity.

But the child defends herself. "But he does, don't you, Jesus?"

She has completely melted his heart. His chest burns with passionate reds and yellows and ambers that are leaping about fiercely and look ready to jump right out of him.

"You are so precious, Little One, and you are so right! Would you like to come and sit on my lap?"

Without a second thought she lets go of her sisters' hands and climbs over their legs to reach him, plonking herself in his lap. She is so willing, so trusting, and so courageous. Jesus gazes upon her with his full attention and some moisture around his eyes. "Thank you for speaking out. What a brave little girl you are."

She is fascinated by the glow in his chest and asks if she can touch it. Or will it burn her? She lays her little hand against his heart. "It's nice and warm!" Her face lights up at her discovery.

"Do you know why, sweetie?"

"Because you loves me!" She gives another giggle and a wiggle. It seems she can't help but talk about his love for her except with delight.

He hugs and squeezes her in his big arms, and her joy escapes in little sighs and crinkles at the corners of her eyes. She snuggles against him.

"Can I put my brokey bits in your heart, Jesus?"

"I would love you to, but it's best if you let me pick them out of your heart because I don't want you to cut your fingers. I will be very careful, I promise. It won't hurt at all."

She looks away as he starts to pick out long, sharp slivers of glass. He places them in his other hand for her to see.

"Why they in there, Jesus?"

Jesus explains that every time people told her she was good for nothing or belittled her, every time they silenced her, falsely accused her, or humiliated her, the stab she felt in her heart was one of these shards of glass piercing her.

He points to other tinier splinters of glass and explains that these were the bits that flew off whenever her parents were arguing, fighting, or abusing each other. Because her heart got in the way of them, they got lodged there. Though they were minute, they were terribly painful. (I start to sense anguish in the children when he says this.)

Jesus checks that all the miniscule shards are removed from her heart, using tweezers for the remaining ones. Then he shows her the pieces in his hand and checks with her that it's OK for him to put them into his furnace. She nods her assent, so he tips them into his chest.

At first the orange glow darkens and deepens, but then it burns stronger and brighter than ever until it is almost pure white.

The little girl is fascinated. She has no pain. She waits to see what will happen next. Jesus reaches into his chest and, like a magician, pulls out a small glass object.

"Here, I believe this is for you!" he says with a wink. "This is what I made out of your broken pieces." He places a little glass swan into her hands. She is enchanted.

"Presie for me?"

She throws her arms around him to hug and kiss him, unable to contain herself.

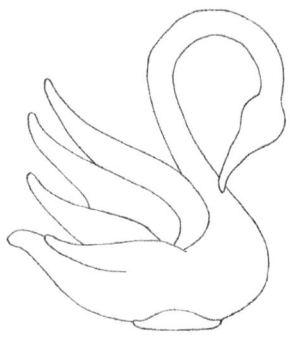

She is a catalyst, this brave little girl, for she unlocks some of the fear in her sisters' hearts, and they too decide to risk trusting the stranger with their pain. He moves around the circle, spending time with each child, carefully removing the glass slivers from their wounded hearts and dropping it into the loving furnace of his own heart, causing those hungry flames to throb and dance. To each child he gives a small glass object—each one different, each one thoughtfully chosen for that particular child. He wants them to know that they matter to him, every single one of them. The younger ones start climbing on his lap, and a couple of the babies are unstrapped from the big girls' backs and are laid in his arms. All of them are keen to be near him, keen to come close to the stranger who has removed such pain from them.

The circle is gone. Now there is something close to a pile of bodies, and at the center is a man with a glowing heart radiating extraordinary love. It was once written that he said, "Let the little children come to me," and today I see it with my own eyes. This man loves children. He treats them with respect and loves them all. He cannot bear for them to be hurting. Their pain is his pain, and he will always help them find their way to health and wholeness if he is given the opportunity to do so. He listens with deep understanding to their concerns, validates their feelings, honours their decisions, and works tirelessly and patiently to win their trust, so they can finally come into a relationship with Love and be set free.

Uncertain One

For me to tell you about Uncertain One, I should first explain double binds and how they affect a child. Wikipedia describes a double bind as "a situation in which a person is confronted with two irreconcilable demands or a choice between two undesirable courses of action." Double binds are difficult enough for adults, but for children they are impossible. Take, for example, that young part of me who faced the "think/don't think" double bind, two conflicting messages from the person in authority over me. As a child I was punished for "not thinking" when I'd done something perceived as bad. "Why don't you think? You never think." On other occasions I was punished for having thought. When trying to explain why I had done a "bad" thing, I might say, "But I thought you said . . .", which might then be met with, "Oh, you 'thought,' did you? Who told you to think? Did I tell you to think?" Double binds put a person in an impossible position and contribute to mental health problems. It is like being stuck between a rock and a hard place with no way out, damned if you do and damned if you don't. This is especially damaging to the brains of children. They do not have the maturity to process or find a way through the two negatives presented.

When Jesus introduced me to Uncertain One, I was shocked to see this child had a wide metal choke collar fastened around her neck. It had chains dripping from it to metal bands around each wrist. Oh, my goodness, it looked barbaric and painful and must have chafed at her young skin. Yet, she appeared largely unaware of it, or perhaps so accustomed to it being there that she did not notice it much anymore. Jesus had already prepared me that this Little One carried the double bind for "think/don't think," so when I saw the medieval harnesses, I realized they were indicators of how the double bind had locked onto her and disabled her.

* * *

Jesus invites her to come sit beside him on the couch and to share her story with him. She is a ten- or eleven-year-old who does not hesitate but strides over, sits down purposefully beside him, and starts to gather her thoughts. She does not seem afraid to be vocal, and she opens up to him surprisingly quickly, though it mystifies me that she makes no reference to her iron manacles. Her concerns seem to be in a different direction altogether.

"Life is so confusing," she laments. "People don't understand me, and I don't understand them. Relationships just don't make any sense to me! I feel so let down and in pain all the time. I'm trapped, alone, and bereft."

Gosh, she's an intense child! All these negative emotions surging through her.

She is looking at Jesus while she talks, and because she's part of me, I can tell she reads nothing but indifference in his face as she bares her soul to him. To her it is obvious that he just doesn't care. Knowing this cannot be true, I turn my attention to Jesus and notice immediately that his face reads alarm and concern, mixed with sadness, compassion, and an obvious desire to help her. I find it both interesting and perturbing that she and I "see" him so differently.

Nevertheless, I know she wants to be free and unshackled. (To my mind comes imagery of her peering over a garden fence with a deep and tangible longing for what is on the other side. The grass is always greener on the other side, as they say, but in this case, it really is. Her yard is bare and filled with trash while the neighboring yard is green and lush.) Yes, she definitely wants out of the confines of her imprisonment, but I also sense that Jesus is the only one who can release her by unlocking that dog collar of double binds and that she would have to be willing for him to do it. I really don't think she trusts him enough for that yet, and my suspicions are confirmed when she matter-of-factly whispers to me, "He's a tyrant, and he treats me worse than a dog!" A peculiar perspective! It certainly does not describe the Jesus I have come to know and appreciate! No wonder she won't allow him to help her.

Jesus and I talk together as I ask him how we should proceed from this impasse. He has a way of remaining calm and patient even during times of deadlock with my Little Ones. He suggests that she might feel safer with me, the adult Fi, than with him and that perhaps I can ease some of her anxiety. He recognizes that I might be able to reach her where he cannot.

Jesus steps back, so I approach her and sit beside her on the other side. I offer her a cautious smile and I hold my hands out to her, not quite knowing what to say. She takes my hands and looks at them, turning them over as she studies them. The chains clink and clunk as she moves. Will these hands hurt her?

"My hands will never hurt you," I say with sincerity.

"They want only to help you and be here for you." She studies my face, looking intently into my eyes for any catch or falseness on my part. But I know what she can see, for I feel it rising to the surface in me. She sees that I am stable, solid, dependable and that I am for her, not against her. Wow! That is really who I am becoming! It is amazing to feel this in myself! I don't know if I really knew it until this moment! Hesitantly, I explain to her that the person I am becoming is all because of that man over there, Jesus. He is the reason I am able to be present to her now as an advocate for her good.

"He's always the same toward me," I explain. "There are no terrifying surprises from him. He always welcomes me, is always happy to spend time with me, and is always rooting for me, encouraging me, and valuing me."

"You are so lucky," she murmurs with a slump of her shoulders.

"He wants to be the same for you too. He's just waiting for you to let him. I promise he is safe, and I promise he will never hurt you. He is the safest person I know—and actually, the least confusing too! You will not find anyone more honest or kind. You can trust him, dear girl. That is the truth."

She turns her attention to him. He remains standing to one side, waiting for her decision. He will not force her, not even to heal her.

She still holds my hands, but dropping one, she stretches out her arm to invite him to join us. And so we stand, the three of us, in a circle holding hands. A small trinity: Uncertain One, me, and Jesus, the chained child now linked to our love and truth on both sides.

I sense I still need to be the one who mediates, so I ask her, "How would you feel about Jesus taking a look at that collar and seeing if he can unlock it? I know he has a key.

I will be here with you. We are safe, dear."

With a nod, her eyes fixed on me and her hand gripping mine, she allows him to undo the heavy collar. Gently and carefully he lifts it away, revealing such raw, chewed-up flesh that I cannot help but wince. We apply soothing ointment to her wounds, taking our time so as not to hurt her. Her wounds are deep, but Jesus reassures us that they will heal over time. She slowly turns her head, first this way, then that. It is a new experience for her to have so much freedom of movement. She sighs as if her load has been lightened.

"May I take a look at your wrists too?" Jesus asks.

She lifts them to him, the thick metal bracelets with chains that now drag on the floor. With ease he undoes them and discards them along with the collar. She will never see them again, never feel their rough edges against her skin. The power of those double binds is finished.

After we have tended her wounds and eased some of her pain, we sit together on the couch and drink hot chocolate. She does not miss the sound of those rattling chains as she lifts the mug to her lips. She does not miss the heavy collar as she gratefully bows her head forward to sip. Her hot chocolate tastes like glorious freedom to her, the best drink she has ever had.

Whilst not wishing to detract from the ease she is now feeling, I can tell that Jesus has something important to say to her. This is something he wants her to carry with her from now on. He presents it to her as two new laws, rules of life that she can live by. These are the laws of "the other side of the fence" where the grass is green. They are laws that will increase her freedom, not limit her. They will teach her to no longer fear authority figures and to begin to know her own value and abilities.

The first law of her new freedom is that she will always

have the right to question him. He will never be offended, and he will welcome her questions whether they are born out of curiosity, resentment, fear, or frustration. He wants her to learn to use her mind and to vocalize what she has until now internalized. Questions are a good thing from here on! They are not going to be avoided or punished. They will help her understand what's going on and how to come to her own conclusions.

The second law of the other side of the fence is that he will never demand, force, coerce, or manipulate her to do anything. He will only invite her, and she will always get to choose whether she wants to or not. Her decisions will never taint or diminish his love for her, a love that is guaranteed for eternity. He will always respect her choices. Others who live by this law and treat her this way will be safe people for her, people she can trust her heart with. This will help her read people better and steer clear of codependency.

My child part returns to the hospital wing of the great house to be taken care of by the angels until all her wounds are healed, and she can just be a girl again, freed forever from the curse of double binds.

Those new laws probably didn't mean much to her back then in the Kindness Room. She was more interested in the sensation of being free of her shackles and the taste of that hot chocolate. But over the course of time, those two laws have become more and more natural and have come to symbolize some of the freedom I live in now.

Living on the other side of the fence is where I was always meant to live, yet it had been so unreachable for the first forty-five years of my life. I have discovered there are others who live by these laws too. These are people who are unchained and who will not enslave others to their need for power or popularity or their agenda. Jesus was wise! He knew what I needed and what would set my feet on a healthier course. Asking questions, discovering my own mind, and learning to be free from obligation in my decision making has radically changed how I relate to God and to others. For this I am so very thankful.

The Helping Ones
(Little Mother and Gentle One)

On this day I got to meet a couple of my little 'helping parts.' I didn't even know such a thing existed! I had been in a season of great distress where my inner turmoil had worn me out and I felt like I was drowning in anguish. To encourage me, one of my Listening Prayer facilitators suggested that we see if there were any Little Helper parts that could assist me in tending and supporting all the Little Ones who were struggling at that time. I had never thought I might have inner children who were healthy and whole, and I was interested to discover who they might be.

* * *

The first one I find is a dear young thing, just a toddler actually and probably only about eighteen to twenty-four months old. She is wearing a cute red tartan skirt held up by straps over a hand-knitted yellow sweater. Her legs are still chubby with baby fat. I can tell straight away that she is a happy little soul, and it comes to me that her name is Little Mother. Her job is to care for her family, namely her parents and her younger siblings. Oh, she loves it! It gives her the greatest joy to take care of them and to do what she can to make their lives easier. I know you would never think a child so young could be a mother, but she has been a mother from the day her baby brother was born when she was just thirteen months old.

She sits with Jesus on the big swing in the garden. It is a beautiful day, a soft wind blowing their hair and warm sunshine on their faces. The garden is green and full of life. How content she is to be with him! He is an old friend, and she feels completely safe and deeply comforted by his closeness. Everything is at peace.

Despite the idyllic setting and her happy temperament, I notice that my dear Little Mother has a hole in her heart. This empty space contains her longing to be loved for *being* who she is, rather than for *doing* all the helpful things she does. Her eyes are full of trust as she smiles up at Jesus. She has a radiance that melts his heart, and mine.

"Come over here, sweetie," he says, as he beckons to his right and another child approaches. To my delight, I recognize her as the One Who Was Once Hidden! Her arms are laden with glittering, shimmering gold dust, her special gift of love to the world. Of course, it spills out everywhere because gold dust cannot be contained in a child's arms, but it keeps refilling as it continually gushes and tumbles out of her loving heart. That is the beauty and joy of it—a glittering, shimmering mess wherever she goes! There are trails of it across the grass. This gold dust is a gift of pure love to Little Mother, and she doesn't have to share it or give any of it away; it's just for her! Piles of it to play in, to throw into the air, to make pictures out of, to rub on her skin, to run through her fingers and toes. She is tickled pink!

Today, she not only gets gold dust, but she also gets

doughnuts from Jesus! A whole plate of them in all her favourite flavors, which happen to be British, of course! Even these she doesn't have to share! She is happily munching and sporting a sugar moustache, her eyes sparkling and her cheeks full. She notices that the hole in her heart is getting filled too!

Little Mother offers Jesus a doughnut, which he takes and eats since he likes British doughnuts too, and soon he also has a white sugar moustache. She chatters to him about how she knows he loves her, and it is only because "I'm me," she says with a twinkle. She really wants to sit on his lap, which, of course, he is delighted to accept. Perched on Jesus's knees, facing him and babbling (in words that only a toddler and Jesus would understand) with waving, expressive hands, Little Mother's heart is fit to burst. Now she knows she is loved for being herself, not just for what she does to care for others!

She will be a safe and nurturing presence for some of my badly wounded Little Ones.

It so happens that I discover another One today. She is more difficult for me to describe, for I cannot exactly see her, but I can sense her. She is like a breeze, a forest fairy, a dancing mist. She is like the flutter of a butterfly's wing and the color of a pink diamond. She is like the fragrance of wild sage or lavender carried on the warm wind of a summer's evening. You see how difficult it is for me to picture her? But this I know: she has been with me all my life. She was present even when I was a newborn baby! Her name is Gentle One, and her gift is that she is able to calm troubled waters.

On this day when she comes to Jesus, he gives her a scepter of authority. This gift is so unexpected, for she is a humble soul and certainly doesn't look for the limelight, but she shyly takes the rose-gold scepter with wonder in her eyes, and she smiles gently into the face of the Christ. Now she can not only calm the rough seas but also, with this scepter, she can part the waters, and there will be a way through where there was once no way. What a remarkable gift! I cannot help but think she will soothe and bring a dose of hope to some of my distraught Little Ones. They will not fear her, for she will approach them so gently.

He also gives her a small, shiny pebble on which are inscribed the words "you count." She will get to carry this with her always, and it will remind her that she matters, that she makes a difference. She has been looked down upon as my weakness rather than my strength for so long, neither valued nor appreciated. Her voice has been an irritation to others, but Jesus reassures her that her voice tickles his ears with pleasure and does not annoy him at all. Hers is a good voice, a much-needed voice, a voice of quiet authority. I can feel her confidence growing. He sees her, he hears her, and he believes in her. His attitude toward her also helps me to realize that she is precious to me after all and that I can not only accept her more comfortably now but also start to really love and appreciate her.

And so, I come to the end of my session of introduction to a couple of my inner Helping Ones. Perhaps this is the beginning of starting to realize that the true nature of my inner children is to be to my support and sanity. I have a growing recognition that my Little Ones are my allies, not my enemies, and that we can form a partnership that will make life so much better for me—for us.

Hopeless One

I had been weepy for days; something must have triggered me. Eventually, one night, I saw Jesus in the padded cell where my little part was being cared for. Her name was Hopeless One, and she seemed to drip tears even while she slept. Until now she had not let Jesus near her.

It may seem odd to have padded cells in the safehouse of my heart. I had not visited these rooms, but I had been aware of them there. I felt they housed the most severely damaged of my inner parts, particularly those who were in danger of self-harm, hurting others, or suicide. I did not know how many there were, but I knew they called Jesus "the jailer," for they knew he had the keys to their cells. In a sense it was true, for I had given him permission to hold the keys to their hearts and their healing. Sometimes I was overwhelmed by their madness—those poor tormented parts churned up such crazy obsessive thoughts and could not be reasoned with. During one or two Listening Prayer sessions, an angel had brought them a sleeping draught to calm them, so we could focus on other Little Ones who were more ready for their healing. I have never thought their padded cells symbolized anything other than great care being taken of them. The soft walls were to protect them from harm and to protect my other vulnerable Little Ones from being targeted by them. I believe that some of my healthy child parts also tended them, with the support of the kind mama angels (who often seemed to be African—perhaps because I spent a portion of my childhood living in Africa, which had felt like home), and I had the distinct sensation that the Helping Ones sang to them and cuddled them as only an innocent child could. Certainly, they would never have entertained any adult approaching them, but possibly another child might.

* * *

"You *never* came to help me through all those years, so why should I trust you now?" her weak voice wails.

Hopeless One is utterly exhausted after this past two weeks of so much distress. Thankfully, Jesus and I are now able to sit with her in the corner of her room. She is a crumpled heap, barely alive it seems, but at least she does not push him away as he nestles her on his lap. Jesus does not try and talk to her; he is very quiet, very still. He just lets her rest in his arms, though every now and again he rocks her a little. Tears leak from her closed eyes without ceasing, and I notice that he seems to be crying too. I know he feels her pain. I have often seen him do this with my Little Ones. Somehow their sorrows are always his sorrows. There is a grieving lament in his chest that reminds me of a haunting melody I once heard played on the Irish bagpipes. When I look up, I note fresh rainbows, in soft pastel shades, painted on the walls of her cell, and I think that perhaps there is new hope rising for this Little One.

We visit Hopeless One a day or two later, and this time we collect her from her padded cell. She is about eight years old. I get to carry her in my arms, for she is so frail and thin. I imagine she feels safer with me than with the one she calls the jailer. I follow Jesus down the stairs to the Kindness Room, where I cradle her on my lap while Jesus builds a fire in the fireplace. Soon its flames are glowing brightly, and the whole space feels warm and cozy. The fire's crackling and hissing are such comforting sounds.

A large African angel mama with a beautiful smile and kind eyes comes in with a tray of hot chocolate for us. We grasp our mugs with both hands and sip.

I am mindful of this child's fears and anxieties. I want her to have a feeling of some control if, and when, she needs it, for I sense that life has afforded her little say in what has happened to her thus far. I spot a pile of cushions on the floor, hidden behind the couch, and I explain that she can go hide there any time she needs to. It's a safe place prepared especially for her. If anything gets too much for her, she can simply run there, no questions asked.

Jesus turns from the fire and sets his gaze on the little girl. He has been pondering what to say, and his words are carefully and tenderly chosen. He gets straight to the point. "I heard your prayers. I heard you every time you called out for me, and I came each time."

Oh boy, she does not like that! I am surprised at the reaction of one who seemed so limp and lifeless a moment ago! She tenses immediately. "You never came!" she screams. "I was all alone!"

Heck, she's calling him a big fat liar! If I wasn't holding her, I think she might gouge his face with her fingernails! Her eyes are a dark, angry blaze of resentment and disgust. I guess she does have some backbone in her after all!

Undaunted, Jesus continues, his voice steady. "I sat in the chair by your bed and watched you sleep every night. And I was there every morning when you awoke. Every moment I was checking to see that you were OK, and I was longing to comfort you."

Hopeless One looks searchingly into my face, frowning deeply with exasperation. "Why is he saying that? Who does he think he is?"

I stare back at her, not knowing how to respond. And then something totally unexpected happens, something neither she nor I are at all prepared for: my father enters the room and walks over to stand by the fireplace. I don't notice his expression or anything particular about him; all I know is that he is here.

The composure of the child in my lap changes instantly. Her anger morphs with lightning speed into cringing distress. Her head is down, her breathing is shallow and racing, and she is crying in painful bursts. She silently, desperately pleads with me that she might go and hide. I usher her to safety behind the couch, and she huddles under the cushions where she cannot be seen. I remain close by her, wondering why my father has come and why he has caused such a reaction.

In the next moment, I see that Jesus has joined us behind the sofa, his presence instantly bringing a feeling of reassurance and grounding to me. He crouches beside the little girl and leans in close to her ear.

"We'll hide together," he whispers as he curls up under the cushions beside her. He lies on his side facing her, close enough for her to see his face and feel his breath on her cheek yet without touching her. "Why are you so upset?" Jesus asks gently, though, of course, he already knows the answer.

I am surprised that she answers, though it takes her a few seconds. "Because even though it's within his power, my dad will not shield or protect me." She is very articulate for a child, and I realize she has thought about this before, and it has weighed on her for a long time.

"All children need a protector," Jesus agrees, nodding. There is something very affirming about the way he says this. He speaks as one who knows, one who was once a child himself and who has the authority of experience. "You know, I would really like to be your shield and protector."

She looks surprised. Her shield and protector? "How will you do that?" she asks.

"Let me show you, Little One," he says as he gets to his feet and extends his hand to her. "Stand up with me!"

Once she is on her feet, he moves to stand behind her, his hands resting lightly on her shoulders and the back of her head to his tummy. She turns her head around to see him there, so tall that he overshadows her. She catches the faintest whiff of something good. Is it his clothes? His skin? Has he been baking bread in the kitchen or simmering Christmas spices in apple cider? The scent lasts for just a moment, but it sticks in her nose, and she can't help but feel drawn to him.

"See? I am much bigger than you and can easily protect you." He smiles down at her with big kind eyes and a soft grin.

She looks puzzled, still not sure if he is trustworthy. "Why would you want to do that?" she asks, turning to face him, so she can see his expression properly.

He doesn't rush to answer her, and when he does his voice is thoughtful and solemn. "Nothing would gladden my heart more than to be your protector. Actually, it's one of my favourite things to do for the people I love." Again, that reassuring smile.

She gulps, struggling for the courage to speak. "You're saying you love me? But you don't know me, so why would you love me?" Her voice is distrustful and small.

He crouches before her. I hold my breath, realizing

this is a significant moment, a holy moment when even time stands still in reverence. "I have always known you," he says, "and I have always loved you."

Her eyes grow big as the engine of her mind churns to figure this out. Finally, "Are you the Creator?" she whispers.

His grin grows as wide and alive as the Fraser River. "Yes! I'm *your* Creator!" His whole body chuckles. How delighted and proud he sounds! I give an involuntary sigh of joy.

There is a long pause as his words sink in. "This is so much to take in," she admits, shaking her head slowly from side to side. "So much!" Then another thought occurs to her. "But how come I didn't know you were there if you really were always there?" She gazes intently at him, her whole face open, waiting for his answer.

"Because you thought I was like him," Jesus says, pointing at my father. "When an accusation or a punishment was coming at you, he would step aside and let its force target you. But I won't do that. I will step in front of you and take the hit for you."

She is still puzzled, stunned, and a little suspicious. "Really? Would you really do that?" Can this be true? Would he really protect her and keep her safe? Would he choose to be her defender?

"Would you like me to do that for you?"

She nods slowly, not taking her eyes off him.

"Then here I am, and I'm not going away. I will *always* be here to do that for you."

Something has shifted in this little girl. Something Jesus said or something about him has changed her view of him. What is left of her reticence and mistrust have evaporated, and she is no longer cautious around him. I guess she must have believed him when he told her he loved her, and perhaps she is seeing that he is different from her father after all. Something about him has done this. In fact, the next thing I see is her putting her arms up to him and Jesus lifting her up into his embrace. Her heart seems to be shouting, "Thank you!" I am amazed! What a transformation from the broken, wailing child I first met in the padded room!

"Now that you've got me," Jesus continues, hugging her tightly, "can you forgive your dad for not coming to help and protect you?"

In the safety and security of his arms, she replies without hesitation, looking at my father, "Yes, I forgive you, Dad. It's OK now that I have Jesus. Don't be sad, Dad. Jesus will take care of me. He will protect me now."

Spontaneously, she slips out of Jesus's arms, runs over to our father, and gives him a brief hug. She smiles at him and waves goodbye as she turns back to her new friend and protector. A moment later, Dad is gone.

Jesus invites her to sit with him on the couch. There is more he wants to tell her. She hops confidently onto his lap, studying his face, her head listing to one side.

"I can see in your face that you have a kind heart," she says, gently pressing his cheeks with her palms.

His face lights up. He wants to talk with her about the rainbows he painted on the walls of her cell. I had seen her tracing them with her finger the other day. "From the first moment you existed, there has been a rainbow over your life," he tells her. Jesus explains that even in the darkest times, rainbows of hope were like banners over her because he always saw and believed there was hope for her future. He even takes us back to some childhood memories where we felt overtaken by despair and hopelessness and shows that he was not only there but was also full of hope for us in the midst of our troubles.

"Thank you, Jesus." This dear child wraps her arms around his neck, kissing him on the cheek. "Please keep saying it's going to be alright." He chuckles at her words. "Could you always hold me in your arms, so I'll always know it's going to be alright? I love you, Jesus."

"I love you too, Little Lamb. And yes, I will always hold you and always let you know it's going to be alright." He continues to hug her close.

We discuss what Hopeless One's new name might be. "Hopeful" seems like an obvious fit, and she seems satisfied with it. "I'd like to be so full of hope that I'm brimming over with enough to give away to others," she says, her eyes now alive and sparkling.

"I'd like that too," Jesus says.

To my mind comes a picture of a large urn acting as a fountain, a garden feature with water flowing over and out of it, rippling down its gently curved sides. Even the sound of it gushing and trickling brings rest.

"Can I be a water feature in your garden, Jesus, making sounds that bring rest to other people's souls?"

Jesus's face is soft with what I can only describe as adoration as he touches her lips with his finger. "You shall speak hope into other people's lives." Then he touches her eyes. "Even when they can't see it, you will see hope for their futures." His fingers rest on her ears. "When doom and gloom is all around them, you will still hear songs of hope." Finally, he puts his hand on her heart. "Hope will always live in here because now you know that I am always here with you." He kisses her on her cheek.

It feels like the right time for her and me to be reunited, so I open my arms to embrace this sweet child, and she joyfully climbs into my heart.

"Welcome home, Hopeful!" I breathe. "I wouldn't want to do life without you!"

I hug Jesus and thank him for all he has done, giving me a sense of hope in a part of my life that had felt utterly hopeless for so long.

We sit together on the sofa a little longer, drinking hot chocolate. He cautions me that I may still feel pangs of hopelessness at times, but that will be connected to other Little Ones and other issues. As for today, he has healed up a big part of my tendency to get trapped in the quicksand of hopelessness. Something good and lasting has happened in my soul that is going to improve my mental health in the days to come.

The Intimidated One

Today, Jesus and I are sitting together in the Kindness Room where he has arranged for us to meet a new child part. He has, once again, built us a fire that is burning nicely and smells so good. I feel relaxed and expectant, and the room is cozy, warm, and inviting, ready for our little visitor. When she arrives I see that she is young, probably just three or four years old. She is dressed from head to toe in a fluffy grey rabbit costume with long pink ears, the hole for her face perfectly framing her round cherub cheeks. She looks as cute as a button, yet her eyes are fearful and wary, suggesting all is not well inside. Her name is "Intimidated One."

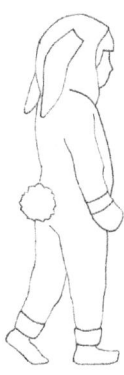

She looks so soft and cuddly in her costume that Jesus is seized by the same desire as me and asks if he can give her a hug. She shakes her head vigorously, stepping back from him and letting us know her thoughts: "Big people are scary!"

"And am I a big person?" he asks. She nods solemnly, her eyes large and apprehensive.

I can tell she is on high alert, absorbing what is going on around her and trying to anticipate what awful thing might happen next. If she can anticipate it, she can prepare herself in some way. It has made her mistrustful of the chance for even one happy experience. For her, there is no safe moment because of the unpredictability of the person who controls and intimidates her little life. Calm dialogue may turn into threatening words and harsh touch that could assault her at any time, though she rarely comprehends the reason. She has concluded, "It is because I'm bad. Somehow, I make people angry. There must be something wrong with me."

Without speaking she warns Jesus, "My heart is very, very black. This costume is just a cover up."

He hears her, of course. By this time, he is down on his knees in front of her, his eyes at her level, his hands in his lap. I can tell that his heart is squeezed tight with compassion and care for this small figure who has learned so young that she contains incomprehensible darkness at her core.

"Even if your heart is so very black," he responds in a calm, tender voice, "I still love and accept you just as you are. I don't mind at all."

Now she is surprised. She was not expecting this! Is he really saying he doesn't mind if there's something wrong with her? How can she trust what he says? And why would it be OK for her to have a black heart?

"Is your costume hot and stuffy inside?" he asks.

"Yes, but I feel safer in here."

She wants him to talk more; he is intriguing to her. She has never talked to anyone like this before, and she finds herself wanting to be honest with him.

"What are you hiding from in there?" he asks.

Aha, he's intuitive too! How did he know she is trying to hide behind the cuddly exterior? And how could she ever explain what or who she is hiding from?

"Big scary monsters," she replies.

Jesus's next question takes me by surprise. I don't see it coming. He has perfectly understood her answer but chooses to take a different tack in order to reach a place of connection with her. If he can't build trust with her, there is little hope of helping her. "Would you be OK if I wear a costume like yours too?"

For the first time I see a smile flit across her face. Somehow his idea has tickled her. Immediately, Jesus is grinning at us while dressed in an adult-sized rabbit costume! It too is grey with enormous pink ears, and he looks quite ridiculous! But she loves it! She jiggles on the spot, her hands covering her mouth. She can't contain herself! He has broken the dividing wall, and she spontaneously climbs into his lap and starts chatting with him, looking eagerly into his face. "You can be the Daddy Rabbit, and I'll be the Baby Rabbit," she says, and she promptly snuggles against his chest, sucking her thumb. She has a whole make-believe game planned out!

He holds her for a little while, quietly and tenderly, then places his hand lightly on her chest. "Let me see . . . Oh, I can feel your heartbeat! I really like your heart, Little One. It makes me happy."

"My heart makes you happy?" She pulls her thumb out and leans away from him, so she can see his face, wondering if he actually means it.

"Yes," he says, smiling. "I can feel it's a good little heart, and I can tell that you are a very good little girl."

She is mesmerized for a moment, letting the words play over in her mind, soak into her being, swish around her insides. Such warmth, such kindness from this stranger, this new friend. How come he sees such goodness in her? It feels like healing medicine to be spoken to in this way.

"How would you feel about getting out of your costume now?" he asks. "You'd be so much cooler and freer without it."

She agrees quite readily, and he helps her out of her rabbit suit. I see she is wearing a dress underneath, and Jesus is back in his usual clothes again. She is still snuggled up on his lap and enjoying feeling so delightfully safe and comfortable and "good."

Needing more reassurance, she takes his hand and places it back over her heart. "How's it feeling now?" she asks, looking up at him.

"Oh, it feels good, very good," he replies. She doesn't want his hand to move, so he sits with her for a long time and lets his hand rest on her chest. As often as she asks, he tells her what a good and lovely little heart she has. She starts to glow.

At one point he turns to me, the adult Fi, who is watching, and he rests his hand on my adult heart and tells me that my heart is good too, very good, and very lovely. How kind his eyes are, how comforting his gaze, how accepting his whole demeanour is. And I see, written on his hand, the word "Approval."

To this day, whenever I lay my hand over my heart, it is as if his hand of approval is laid over top. My heart is good, very good, and very lovely.

The Lake of Sorrows

There is a garden in my heart that I like to visit sometimes. Jesus is the gardener there, and he is creating a beautiful landscape. It has many overflowing flowerbeds and lawns, secret walled gardens, wild meadows, orchards, and hidden spots to rest and enjoy the beauty of the plants, trees, and vistas.

One day when I am walking in the garden, I discover it has a huge lake in it. Unlike the rest of the garden though, I can tell straight away that this is not a peaceful or happy place. As I look out across the lake, I have an uneasy feeling of disquiet that makes me want to retreat.

I ask Jesus about the lake and its history. Where did it come from? Why does it emit this brooding dark feeling? He explains to me that it is a "Lake of Sorrows" and that it has taken many years to form. Its waters are made up of my tears.

There is a small pebble beach, and there I sit while Jesus stands on the water, the sunshine bright behind him. I wait to see if he wants to tell me about this Lake of Sorrows. I suspect he has brought me here for a reason.

He reassures me that I don't need to be afraid, (how often he says this to me!), for this lake will teach me things about myself that he feels sure I am ready to learn. As always, he reminds me that he will be with me as these truths come to light. Then he explains that when the right time comes, he will remove this lake and build something much better in its place.

"Well, why is it here?" I ask, playing with the pebbles to distract myself while I await his answer. Let's get on with this, please!

He squats in front of me, still with his feet on the water, but now we are face to face. "Because this is how you coped with life, Fi, but it does not need to be this way anymore."

"But how did I cope with life? What do you mean exactly?"

"You absorbed grief, distress, and sadness from all around you and horded it inside. At first it was a puddle, then a pond, and finally it grew to be an ever-expanding lake."

I can't say this comes as a big surprise. Nevertheless, it is strange and uncomfortable to hear it spoken so clearly, especially with my new awareness of the lake's ominous presence. I have been called a "burden bearer" for many years and have to confess that I have drawn some of my identity from this trait, the Fi who empathizes and carries other people's suffering in her heart. The growing realization that this may not be entirely healthy, that it may even be grotesquely unhealthy, is not something I feel very happy about!

"Was I born with a bit of sorrow already inside me, Jesus?"

He sighs, his eyes kind. "Indeed you were, Fi, indeed you were."

This consoles me somewhat. I am comforted that the lake isn't entirely my own doing, brought about through my tendency toward codependency and my melancholic, pessimistic nature! It makes sense that I've always leaned toward compassion for others and also that I've inherited some of my penchant for sadness through my DNA.

"So, you're saying I've been kind of a sponge for sadness, Jesus?"

He smiles and turns to look behind him at the waters that stretch far into the distance. "There have been times when you have camped out at this lake for days on end, and it was as if it was all you could see. Those were dark times of depression and gloom." He looks back at me. "Do you remember those times, Fi?"

I know he is right. I have set up my tent here during some seasons and focused exclusively on the overwhelming suffering of others. I think it has been my way of relieving my sense of helplessness at my inability to alter or alleviate their trials. Sometimes I've also felt guilty that my life has been so much easier than theirs. By absorbing their sadness, I feel I am identifying with them and somehow standing in solidarity with them. It is the best I can offer, but I can see now that it is not very satisfactory for me or for those I am wanting to love and care for.

"What shall we do with this lake, Jesus?"

He stands up, turns, and hesitates for a moment. "First, I want to take you for a walk. There are some things I want to show you. Will you come with me, Sweet Fi?" He stretches out his hand to me.

"What, you mean I get to walk on water with you?" Like most people, I have always fancied walking on water!

He laughs. "Come on," he says, then pulls me to my feet. Still holding my hand, he leads me across the water's delicate skin. It is not nearly as difficult as I had imagined. The water gathers itself to become solid under our feet and then turns fluid again as we lift our weight to move forward. After a few steps it feels almost natural.

"What do you notice?" he asks after we have walked a little way out.

The first thing I notice is the breeze. Normally, I would love a breeze, especially if it's warm or refreshing, but this breeze doesn't feel like that at all. Instead, it is cold, clinging, and unpleasant. It wraps itself around me and seeks to blow right into me, hunting for a spot in my interior where it can lodge. It is like a dark, moaning spirit that carries the cries of weeping children on its breath. A shiver runs through me.

"This wind belongs to the lake," he explains. "You won't find it anywhere else. I intend that it should go with the lake when the lake is gone. Would you be OK with that, Fi?"

"Oh yes, that's fine with me!" I hug his arm. The lake feels creepy now. I don't like it. I can't see the bottom, and I wonder what might be hiding under the surface. I have never liked not being able to see to the bottom whenever I have swum or boated; it has always frightened me. But Jesus insists that I am safe with him and that we need to walk farther.

He leads me several hundred metres across the water to a cave where the hillside juts out into the lake. I wouldn't know it was there if I didn't know how to find it; it is so well hidden in the rockface. We enter it, still walking on the water, and it smells just like one would expect, cold, dank, and musty, with sounds of dripping and lapping. Once inside I am surprised to discover that it is lit with small candles placed on any available natural ledges and surrounding a huge stone statue whose name immediately comes to me "Goddess of Self-Pity." I do not like her one bit! She has many tentacle-like arms, and her eyes, though made of stone, drip unceasingly with tears. This place is grotesque. I ask Jesus what it means.

His face is sad, and his words are solemn though not unkindly spoken. "You have bowed the knee before this goddess, knelt before her, and kissed her feet. You have pleaded with her for peace and built your life around her. But, my Dear Fi, she is a death trap, and she will never give you the peace you seek."

It is true; self-pity is one of the ugly and embarrassing aspects of my life. I see now how unhelpful it has been to me, for it has taken on proportions that have been immortalized in the image before me. I kneel before Jesus and close my eyes to pray. I ask him to forgive me, and I renounce the idol of self-pity that I have created. I ask him to help me find a new way of living with my suffering. It is a short and simple prayer.

When I open my eyes, Jesus and I are still on the lake, but the grotto is gone. All that is left is a wall of rock. In the middle of the rock is a gas lamp that is alight with an eternal Flame of Hope, a light that cannot be extinguished. Jesus is standing beside me as we drink in the sight. Hope has been an elusive concept in my life thus far. For there to be a permanent marker of hope in the landscape of my heart feels almost too good to be true. But there it is! And there is more, for Jesus places in my left hand a lantern. He takes some of the flame from the gas lamp to light it. My heart feels so warm and grateful, for though the lake is still dark and cold, we are standing in a little puddle of light, a pool of "hope light" that I get to carry wherever I go.

Jesus is smiling at me, a big, broad grin focused below my chin. Curious, I look down and, to my astonishment, I discover that a warm orange glow is radiating from my chest! It shines out through my clothes, so I guess I must also be pretty bright with hope light inside!

"Please don't let this flame ever be snuffed out," I whisper.

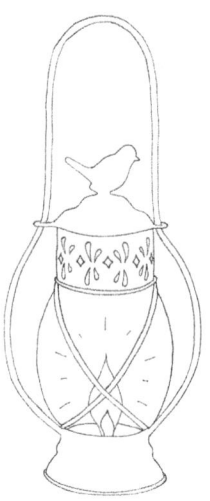

Now we are walking farther on the lake, wrapped in the golden splash of hope light. Jesus still holds my hand. I like his hands; they are kind and strong, and they give me the most reassuring feeling when I place my own hands in them. They steady me and make me feel solid and real, something I struggle to feel most of the time. I wonder what he will show me next.

At some point my attention is drawn to my feet, and I start to notice that below them, under the water's surface, images are floating, moving in and out of focus. Children's faces stare up at me, wild-eyed and voiceless. Hundreds upon hundreds of them. These are all those suffering children whose lives have crossed mine. Not necessarily even in-person, perhaps simply via the TV or in a book or a movie or just passing by, but their torment and anguish had impacted me. Somehow, it entered me and got lodged in my heart. Their images are all alive in me, trapped in the unending pain of the moment I encountered them. It feels like a living cemetery or worse, a pit of hell just beyond the reach of my toes. It is a terrible experience to see them, and I cry.

"Jesus, what is this?" I sob. "Why are these children's faces in the lake?"

"Because you have taken them into your heart, and you thought you could carry their sorrows for them."

"But there are so many of them, Jesus. I don't know who they are anymore, and I don't know what their sorrows are."

"No, you don't, Dear Child. And you never could carry their sorrows for them. That is not your job, but it is mine! I know each of them by name, and I know their sadness and suffering. The truth is, Fi, I wanted to show you the children's faces first, but there are many other faces in this lake—adults and old folks, sick people and abused people—a great company whose suffering affected you. The lake has had to keep on growing to accommodate them all. See how far it stretches?"

I see the lake must be a few miles long. It is a truly desolate place, a nightmare in real time from which there is no escape. I am thankful for that wee lantern I am holding, shining out its hope light, for without it I think I might falter and collapse. The enormity of the disaster I have created within me is too much for me to bear.

"Jesus, what can I do to get rid of all this?"

Thankfully, Jesus knows it is time, I am ready, and there can be no delay. He has been waiting for me to ask him to help him with this for a long time. First, he shows me how there are strings, like fishing lines (super strong and transparent) attaching my heart to each of these suffering ones under the water. With my permission he cuts those strings with his sword. (I didn't even know he carried a sword!) It doesn't hurt. It's like snapping the greens off a bunch of fresh carrots. His blade severs my unhealthy attachment to all those who suffer. It is a clean cut, left then right, right then left, again and again across the length and breadth of the lake until all those invisible threads are broken and have fallen into the water to join their owners.

Next, he asks me to give him the names of all these people I've been carrying in my heart, telling me they don't belong to me; they belong to him. So, I put all their names in a big basket, and I hand it to him. To my surprise he eats them! Every last one of them! He takes them into himself, so they become part of him. There is not one name left for me to carry. The basket is empty, and my heart is freer.

Finally, the time has come for Jesus to drain my Lake of Sorrows and to remove the dark presence that broods over it. I ask him how he will do this. He tells me he will drink it! There was once a cup of suffering that he drank to the dregs, so he knows how to swallow all my sorrows. I am ready for him to take them. All the years of carrying them have been wearying and have robbed me of so much joy. I am so happy to let go of them!

And he does. He drinks my lake dry, so there is no more backlog of tears left. It is all emptied. No wonder Isaiah called him "a man of sorrows, acquainted with grief" (Is. 53:3). He truly understands our sadness and our suffering, and he is able to carry it all.

This aspect of my past is in his care now. All the sadness of my childhood and young adulthood is carried by him. Even the sorrows I inherited from my parents and grandparents and my ancestors before them. He is setting me free. It is becoming easier to let go of my self-pity, and the "dark brooding" over my life is becoming lighter. Day by day he is teaching me how to love and care for others in their sorrows and sufferings without them lodging in my heart in unhealthy ways. I am learning how to give them to him, to let him carry their burdens.

* * *

There is more to this story.

Once the lake was dry Jesus showed me how the bedrock under the lake was like a deep fissure. The bedrock was called "shame," and my early life experiences had helped form the perfectly shaped gouge in the landscape of my heart for the tears of sorrow to collect and form a water mass.

It took some more journeying with him for that shame to start to melt away and the scenery of my heart to begin to heal. But the time came when that deep wound had become just a little valley with a bubbling brook, and, true to his word, Jesus did build a new thing there. He turned it into a peaceful garden where we could walk and talk. He called it "Fi's Prayer Groves," and he filled it with many plants and trees that represented all the different people and situations I pray for. A fruitful and lovely place, free of burdens. A place of rest and hope light.

Meeting the Twins

I had been becoming aware of a new part. She had been sending messages through my mind over and over with thoughts of what she would want to say to certain people who had offended her. This was triggering memories of childhood events where she had been misunderstood and falsely accused, but she had been incapable of addressing them properly at the time.

So, in my mind, I pictured her at a coffee shop where she might be able to talk with a friend of mine about an occasion recently when he had offended me. He had made judgments about me based on hearsay (though meant kindly), but he forgot to check with me for my side of the story before he made his recommendations. My child part had felt thoroughly humiliated and betrayed.

It was only then, when I gave her this imaginary opportunity, that I began to actually see her, a child of about seven years old, standing in a large, empty, sun-baked field.

* * *

The first thing I notice is how short her dress is, exposing her knees. Instantly, I know that her knees hold all her fear and that she is using all her willpower to keep them from crumpling underneath her. Yet her face, though pale, is set like stone, a striking mask that gives nothing away of what I know is racing in her heart.

She is all alone and extremely vulnerable, exposed to violent winds and rain. Wearing only a simple cotton dress, short socks, and shoes, she has no protection from the cold and the wet.

There she stands, resolute and still. Like a lamb before its shearers, she makes no protest, no verbal complaint. Her heart is steeled, for she knows there is no benefit in resisting what is coming. In fact, assuming a position of passivity and accepting that which will terrorize her may help it to pass more quickly. Yet I can tell that she feels sick to her stomach in its dreadful anticipation.

Why is she out there in that vulnerable space?

I hear the screech that summons her, the voice that sets her knees knocking. An unholy bellowing.

"Fiona! Get here now!"

The sound of this woman's voice is terrifying; even an adult might gulp.

My understanding of the role of this part slowly dawns when I become aware that there, cowering in a dark corner, is her counterpart, her twin sister, if you like. My "Brave Front" is that part of me that the world gets to see when I face a frightening trial, and she is the protector and shield of the other part of me who holds the swell and surge of all the underlying feelings. This twin child, her face stricken with terror and tears, is pressing her body into the smallest form she can manage, curled up and trying to be invisible. She, Traumatized One, carries all the emotions that flood her during experiences that frighten her. Such emotions are unacceptable to her mother and need to be kept hidden away, or she risks greater punishment. There is no possible way that this Little One could make it out into that place to which the voice commands her, so her sister, Brave Front, is the one who goes to face the music.

Now that I have this new understanding, it is time for us to meet together in the Kindness Room: me, Jesus, and the twins. Brave Front stands in front of the fire waiting to meet Jesus. Traumatized One is huddled in a corner, barely visible in the shadows. I am filled with pity as I watch these forlorn creatures. My heart could break. Jesus seems to know that the one in the corner is unable to endure an encounter. Although he is fully aware of her and her distress, he turns his attention to her sister.

"You wanted to speak with me?" Brave Front murmurs.

Her face is blank, but her eyes betray her anxiety, and I see her pulse throbbing like an express train in her throat. She is certain she is in trouble. Jesus is silent, quieted by sadness. I imagine he can even smell her fear. He moves slowly toward her. Bending low he sits on the floor in front of her but not too close, so as not to alarm her. He has a small grey bunny in his arms, which he strokes gently and affectionately. He nuzzles it to his cheek, touches its nose to his, and takes his time playing with it, knowing that Brave Front is watching him . . . and wondering. It's such a pretty little rabbit.

Suddenly, I see a large snake slithering past him with the intention of biting the little girl. He tucks the bunny into his lap, grabs the snake with both hands, wrings its neck, and throws it into the fire. His eyes look mad; there is no way he would let it hurt her. Perhaps she needed to see that.

The child gasps and draws back for a moment, but once the snake is gone, she returns to her original stance, waiting for what will surely come, her eyes downcast.

Jesus pulls a burnt stick from the fire, black with soot,

and uses it to write on the stone hearth. He is still seated, so I lean over his shoulder to see what he has written. It says, "Ask me a question."

(I remember the other day he had said to one of my other parts, the Uncertain One, "You may always question me.")

I see the question in her mind, but her lips don't move.

"What do you want [with me]?"

"I want to know you," he replies without a moment's hesitation.

Again, she catches her breath, her eyebrows raised. This is not the answer she was expecting. She takes a moment to compose herself.

"You're lying," forms in her thoughts. "You just want to draw me out, so you can hurt me deeper." A tear creeps down her cheek. She ignores it as she waits, bracing herself for his response.

"No, you're wrong. I really do want only to know you."

He looks suddenly tired, weary, and burdened. My heart goes out to him. I stand behind him and place my hands on his shoulders. I bow my head and pray with him. Not with words but with a silent ache in my heart that echoes the ache in his heart. We ache, him and me, for this poor broken child.

Then he seems to gather himself. The time of intercession is over, so I step back.

"Before you go," he says to the girl, "I'd like to give you a gift."

She stiffens as he leans toward her. She can smell him now. Green grass and fields... and freedom. He does not wait for a reply; he just puts the grey bunny into her hands.

"Would you take care of her for me?" He does not seem to expect an answer.

The interview is over; the children are gone from the room. We do not speak. He sits on the sofa, and I go to sit beside him, tucking my feet up under me and resting my head against his shoulder. This last week he has been the "I AM Peace," so that is what I lean into. He is my peace, and I entrust these two small, wounded children, Traumatized One and Brave Front, to him and his peace.

Traumatized One (Part 1)

Traumatized One was part of a duo. She and her sister had worked together to survive the traumas of my childhood. I had the impression that this Little One carried all the emotions of trauma by hiding away, so that her sister, Brave Front, could go out into that terrifying world and face "what was coming to her" with a deadpan face.

* * *

I see her in the Kindness Room. She is in the far corner, trying to hide in the shadows. She looks very small because she is huddled up like a ball. "Deformed" is the word that comes to mind. Her body has been contorted for so long it is now permanently misshapen. I wonder if she is even capable of standing up anymore.

She looks pitiful, dirty, and unkempt, a bag of nerves, full of anxiety, fear, and involuntary twitches. It must be impossible for her to care for herself; she is in so much pain. I'm sorry to say that she makes me think of Gollum. I'm not sure I could ever love her, and I certainly don't want to go near her. She might attack me in her terror! Yes, she looks terrorized. In fact, she looks mad with fear, and she makes tiny whimpering, moaning noises. She has been overcome (quite literally) by the traumas she has endured.

"Jesus, what can we do for this Little One?" I don't say it out loud, but I know he hears the question in my mind. I am sitting with him on the couch. He has made no attempt to approach the child. Even I can see it would be pointless and might cause her more distress. I wonder if there is any hope for her.

"We will pray for her," Jesus says.

I rest my head on his shoulder and remember that this week I have been thinking on him as "I AM Mercy." It is his mercy that I lay my head against, and it is his mercy that I rest in for this Little One. I sing quietly to myself an old Vineyard song, "Mercy is falling, is falling, is falling. Mercy is falling like soft spring rain . . ."

The tiniest drops of fine, misty rain start to fall on the child in the corner. Gently, so very gently it falls. When she notices, she rubs her skinny arms, and this causes her grime to smear. But as it keeps falling, I see that it is slowly cleaning her. It dawns on me that she actually wants to be clean! That surprises me. I don't know why, but I had assumed she preferred being dirty, yet now it's clear that she would much rather be clean.

As she uncurls herself a little to rub her skin with the wetness, I get to see her body. Her heart must be enlarged because that side of her chest is twice the size of the other, her ribs sticking way out to cover it. She really is quite deformed. One could almost say she is "all heart." I can't help but stare at it; it's so big.

Her face is upturned, letting the raindrops fall on it, her eyes closed. I think she is enjoying it. Even her little face is becoming clear, her cheeks as pale as ice under the muck. It's hard to tell now what are tears and what is rainwater.

I remember how much I love my hot shower each morning. It is sometimes the only peaceful moment of the day, and it is always a pleasure. I look at Jesus. "Did you make that rain warm for her?"

He smiles back at me and winks.

"Oh, thank you, Jesus," I whisper.

Eventually the rain stops. I notice big, velvety white towels piled close to her. She reaches out and pulls one around her. Now she is just a fluffy ball with nothing but a tiny face to see, her wet hair matted to her head.

Jesus indicates to me that this is all this Little One should experience for today. The interview is over, and she is gone from the room. Pools of water remain on the floor in the corner where she was crouched.

"Shall I mop up?" I ask.

"No, I'd like to do that." I can see that he cares deeply for her, that his heart is tender toward her, that it saddens him that he cannot approach her yet because of her great fear. He soaks up all the water in the remaining towels, then holds the bundle in his arms, hugging it to his chest as if he is embracing all of her dirt and tears. He kneels in her corner, his face to the wall, the bundle in his arms. I just watch him. It feels like another of those holy moments.

Then, I don't know why, but I start to sing again. "Mercy is falling, is falling, is falling . . ." The rain starts up again, but this time the drops are much bigger, and they splash all over Jesus's head, shoulders, and back. He lifts his face to receive the rain, and then it just pours down on him. I see his shoulders shaking, and for a moment I wonder if he's weeping, until I hear his big, beautiful laugh. The more he laughs, the more it rains. He looks like a drowned rat!

"Come over here!" He beckons to me with a ridiculous grin, and I slowly, perhaps a little reluctantly, make my way over to stand under the downpour with him. Now he is really chuckling as he stretches his arms wide and welcomes the torrent. I'm not sure what to make of it, being rather a serious person, not given to fits of hilarity, so I stay close to him and just let it wash over me. It is lovely and warm, and I have a tantalizing feeling that something good is coming for my little Traumatized One.

Traumatized One (Part 2)

Some days later I am invited back to the Kindness Room for Jesus's second interview with the little Traumatized Girl. I see that she is still wrapped in that big fluffy towel. She has found it comforting, and she seems more at ease than when last we met. Knowing her fragility, Jesus suggests that we let her receive more mercy rain in her corner before we do anything else. I can tell she enjoys it because she wriggles free of her towel and lifts her face, eyes closed, to let the warm spray of fine droplets touch her skin. A hint of a smile plays on her lips. She smooths her hands over her arms and legs as they glisten with moisture. She looks quite clean now, pale but clean.

Jesus approaches and asks if he can wrap her in a fresh towel. He squats down to gently scoop her into his arms and carries her to the couch, where he sits next to me. She sits quietly on his lap, a small curled-up ball, and allows him to rub her body with the soft towel. I don't think she has ever been touched before, not by hands that won't hurt her. This new experience is extraordinary for her, but she is braver now than last time. I see her looking at him, her eyes searching his for some understanding of why he would care for her like this. He holds her gaze, unblinking, looking deeply into her eyes and letting her see deeply into his. His eyes are innocent, straightforward, and kind holding neither accusation nor malice. They say, "I'm here for you Little One." I think she is starting to melt.

I am sorry to admit it, but, in my eyes she is still rather an ugly child. Perhaps it's her deformed chest, so unusually large on the one side, perhaps it's her bent-up, crooked body. Honestly, I don't think Jesus sees like me at all! All he sees is a small child ready for love and freedom.

He has a dress for her with blue flowers on it and a white collar and, best of all, it's brand new! No one has ever worn it! Oh, she likes that! She lets him put it on over her head. Though it's rather full and tent-like over her curled-up shape, she looks down at it with something close to wondrous joy on her face as she caresses it with her fingers.

Jesus waits some time before he broaches the subject of her trauma. We both know it will be difficult for her to talk about, but we also know it needs to be taken care of somehow. His approach is simple: he would like to carry all her pain for her and give her something way better in exchange.

I suppose I am not surprised that she immediately shrinks back, her little body shaking like my puppy does when I'm taking him to the vet. Just remembering past traumas is traumatic for her. Plus, her whole identity has been wrapped up in the role she has played as the one who carries the emotions of my childhood traumas for me. I imagine she is afraid of losing that. Who will she be if she no longer plays that part?

"Well," Jesus says, "You will have a new identity. You will be the Giver of Gifts."

As he talks to her, my mind throws up images triggered by the expression "Giver of Gifts." I picture my youngest son as a toddler picking dandelions for me. How I loved his innocent, affectionate gestures! Those flowers were a precious gift, and his tender heart was a treasure to me. As I am recalling this happy memory, I know that Traumatized One is watching those pictures shooting across the screen on the back of my brain, thinking, "I wonder what it would be like to touch someone's heart like that little boy does. Just imagine having something good to offer other people. Just imagine being a blessing and a delight!"

Instantly, a carpet of buttercups grows up around us. She is getting the chance to practice on me! Jesus holds her hand and helps her to stand, to walk, and to pick flowers. I can tell she is anticipating bringing delight to someone, to me, and it is making her somehow more attractive. When her hands are full, and the gift is ready, I see her hesitate, afraid to approach me. But Jesus reassures her that it will be OK. He will come with her, and I will love her gift. She timidly places the buttercups into my lap. I smile into her little face and tell her how much I enjoy this beautiful present. I love flowers, and I love yellow! I see a little smile. She looks up at Jesus as if to say, "It worked!"

Jesus returns to the couch, and she is back on his lap, her head resting against his chest and his arms around her.

"I've never felt like this before," she whispers. She is savouring this moment—someone to love her, the chance to give a gift, the feeling that she is a blessing to somebody. It is a lot to take in, a whole new set of unfamiliar emotions.

But Jesus is not finished yet. He explains that if she can give him all the trauma in her heart, she will have so much more room in there for storing gifts, which she can give to whomever she chooses. She is listening and weighing everything he says.

"The best gift you can give me today," Jesus continues, "is all that hurt in your heart. Trust me, Little One, I'd love to carry it for you. It's been such a heavy weight for you to bear, like a Pandora's box full of darkness and dread."

She reaches her small hands into her heart and pats the black box. "It's full of my sorrows as well," she says and then sighs. "I'd like you to take those too. But just hold me one last time before we take it out," she begs.

He rocks her in his arms, humming a little tune. "It's going to be alright, sweetie."

She takes courage from him, her fear subsiding. "I'm ready, Jesus."

Together, they lift that box out, dripping with dark goo all the way. He opens a door in his heart and places the box on an altar inside.

"Thank you," he says, smiling at her. Then, with a spray bottle and a cloth, he cleans out the space in her heart, just like the inside of a microwave. "Now that's a nice place to hold something new!"

I can tell she is a burden bearer, for she is starting to worry about him carrying her Pandora's box of trauma. She places her small hand on his heart and wants to know if the box is going to hurt him or weigh him down.

"Thank you, Little One. Your thoughtfulness touches me, but don't worry. Come, take a look inside my heart again."

She pulls open the door to his heart, only to find that the black box is gone, and in its place is a large treasure chest. Her face shows surprise. With a chuckle Jesus explains that he made her with such a big heart so that this treasure chest could fit inside! It is full of gifts that she will be able to give away and share with others. She is speechless, unable to take it in! What a strange and wonderful day this has been! Now she wants it all, and she welcomes the treasure chest as he slides it neatly into her heart. It fits perfectly.

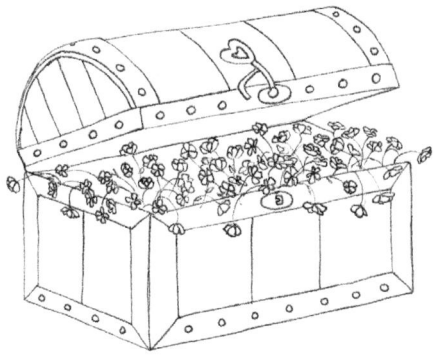

Pausing, he looks into her face. "Always remember it came from my heart."

She nods solemnly, then places her hand over her own heart, feeling a new, warm sensation inside.

She rests against Jesus, tired but oh so happy. They sit quietly for a long time. She has fallen completely in love with him, his kindness, his goodness.

Suddenly, she sits up. 'Where will I live now if not in the corner?"

A picture of a meadow immediately comes to my mind. A child is playing in it, and it's full of wildflowers, butterflies, and sunshine. This will be her playground and her safe place. She wears a string of tiny shells around her neck and her new blue dress. Finally, she looks free and easy with herself. Jesus gives her a drink full of fizzy bubbles. A little belch escapes and makes her giggle. What a sweet sound! It's the first time I've heard her laugh. She drinks some more, so she can burp again. I can see now that her whole body is content and satisfied. She feels safe because she knows she can run into his arms anytime she wants. He is there in the meadow with her. Her chest is still larger than what one would call "normal," but I know

now that that is because she has a huge heart that is full of treasures. Softly blushing light radiates from it whenever she gives them away.

I have to admit, she really is quite lovely now, even beautiful. I am going to enjoy living from the freedom of the meadow instead of the terror of the dark corner. We have a journey together ahead, and I am looking forward to accompanying her on it.

Brave Front

It was only after Jesus had taken care of the Traumatized One that I got to see Brave Front again. This time although she was still the one who stood in the big open space, she was clothed rather differently, and she held herself with greater confidence. She wore a lovely animal-hide dress with tassels, feathers, and beadwork and matching moccasins on her feet. Her hair was now raven black and braided into two long plaits that hung forward over her shoulders and swished from side to side as she moved.

* * *

In my mind I transport her to the Kindness Room where Jesus is waiting. He greets us warmly with hugs and kisses on our cheeks, and we stand back and admire his soft leather aboriginal robes and moccasins. His hair is beautiful, thick and dark, a glossy mane flowing down his back. Brave Front is tickled pink with their new looks, and they can't help but smile at each other.

Jesus invites her to join him on the floor, where they sit cross-legged, facing each other. I take my place on the old couch and watch to see what will happen next.

Jesus is holding a peace pipe, which he has pulled out

of his robe to show her. It is laid across his hands—a long, thin stem and a small round cup to hold the tobacco at the end. It too has feathers and tassels hanging from it and is quite lovely.

I'm a little surprised when I hear him say he'd like them to smoke the peace pipe together! He seems to be quite serious, but the girl may need some convincing.

"Am I old enough?"

"Yes," he replies confidently. "I think you're old enough to handle it."

I am inclined to question his decision, as she is only seven after all! But then I think of all the grown-up and serious situations she has faced in her short life, and I realize he is probably right.

"This will be a symbol of peace between us. You will know that I have come to this meeting in peace, and I will know that you have come in peace too. We will listen respectfully to each other, and we will know that we are heard."

She nods.

Jesus starts puffing on the pipe, getting the gnarly dried leaves in the little cup to burn orange and to make smoke. (I have always liked the smell of a pipe. I believe my father smoked one occasionally when I was young.) Once it is glowing nicely, and its earthy, fragrance is filling the room, he hands the pipe to her. She puts it cautiously to her lips and takes some tentative puffs. She is quite good at it for a novice, though it makes her eyes watery, and she coughs a bit. But I think she is enjoying the invitation to a "grown-up" interaction. She returns the pipe to him, and they take turns puffing. Jesus even blows smoke rings. She likes that!

Then, when it is his turn to hold the pipe, he introduces a new element to the game.

"When I am holding the peace pipe, I may wish to speak something to you, something on my mind, something that is bothering me or something I'd like to share with you, and you will listen. Then I will hand you the pipe, and you may speak something that you are thinking about or concerned about, and I will listen. But we will only speak when we are holding the peace pipe, and the other person will always listen and know that we come in peace."

She listens to the rules with full concentration and bobs her head. She understands. He is teaching her how to communicate with an adult as an equal and without needing to feel threatened or afraid. And so, he starts the process. "Let's give it a go."

He sucks on the pipe, lets the smoke rings rise until they disappear, then pauses while he thinks for a moment. She is on the edge of her seat waiting to hear what he will say. After a while he points to a flowerpot on the windowsill containing some drooping pansies. "I have been worried about my flowers. They don't seem to be doing very well lately."

It sounds a little lame to me! But Brave Front is giving him her undivided attention and has absolute trust in him. She glances across. She has something to say. It's on the tip of her tongue, but she waits her turn. She is getting the hang of this! He hands her the pipe.

"Perhaps your flowers need some water, Mister Big Foot!"

Wherever did she get that name for him? I suppress a chuckle, not wanting to make her self-conscious when she is looking so serious. She pushes the pipe back to him.

"Well, I never thought of that!" he responds with fake astonishment and a warm smile of appreciation. She giggles and jiggles; she can't help herself. He snaps his fingers, and an angel (dressed in similar garb) appears with a watering can and begins to water the flowers. Within moments they are sitting bolt upright in the pot, their sunny faces bright and joyful again.

Jesus is still holding the peace pipe, so, technically, it is still his turn to speak. She holds herself ready as he looks her full in the face. "And how are the flowers doing in your heart, Little One?" he asks gently.

Brave Front drops her head, looks inside her chest, and swallows. Slowly, she takes the pipe back from him. "I think they're just about dead in there, Mister."

She is shocked at her own honesty, that she has let such a revealing detail slip out, but she continues falteringly. "Nothing can really grow in there anyway. It's way too dry and burnt up."

He listens, his head tilted to one side, his expression tender.

It may sound odd, but to me it's as if the landscape in which I had first discovered her—that empty, arid space—is not only a picture of the tormented habitat of her role during my childhood but also a picture of the barrenness within her heart. It interests me that she not only describes it as dry but also burnt. All that had once tried to grow in her heart had been baked to a crisp in the overbearing heat of accusation and judgement before finally withering and dying. Her inner being had become a desolate wasteland.

She is quiet, but when she glances up at him, his eyes seem to be inviting her to say something more.

"Do you think anything could ever grow in here?" she whispers faintly as she glances down at her naked heart. Jesus smiles.

A few days later, we meet again. I had been keen to see what would become of Brave Front. She had made such strides in trusting Jesus and finding her voice. Their last interview had left me hanging.

We gather in the Kindness Room once more. Brave Front wears the same attire as in our last encounter, a stunning aboriginal dress and moccasins and two long black plaits. Jesus is in full regalia this time, with a magnificently beaded, white-feathered headdress. He looks very grand and not just a little intimidating. He is obviously a tribal chief and a person of real authority, but Brave Front doesn't seem perturbed. She looks into his face and is met with that same kind gaze that she has come to know and trust. He winks at her and removes his headdress, placing it to one side. They sit down cross-legged facing each other and prepare for their "peace talks."

He hands her the peace pipe. She takes a quick puff, then gratefully begins to chatter to him about the bunny he had given her previously. She has been taking good care of it and enjoying its softness and cuteness. She is anticipating all that will unfold today. "Do you have something to share with me, Mister?" She hands him the pipe, her eyes fixed on his face, wide and eager.

"I'm so glad to meet with you again, Little One. You have looked after my rabbit wonderfully. Thank you so much. I have been watching you and feel so proud of how you are learning to communicate with others. I love hearing your voice! Today I have more peace to share with you, and I have been so looking forward to our time together. There's something I want to ask you. I know it will be hard, but I also know you are very brave. So, is it OK for us to talk about the dead flowers in your heart?"

He reaches out to take her hand in his, for she has started to cry. There has been so much loss and pain in her heart that it is a relief beyond words that he knows about it and that he cares. He is so respectful, just letting her hand sit in his and allowing her time to gather herself.

"Mister, is there any way these dead flowers can grow again?" she asks, her lips trembling.

"First, we need to talk about what died, my dearest," he responds with gentle gravity. "The truth is that it was your self-worth that died. It is not that you forgot your worth, so don't blame yourself for forgetting. You were never taught it. When we grow up thinking we are a nothing and a nobody, we don't know that we can 'be' or even that we exist or that we can have a voice, opinions, and feelings. But when we grow up knowing we are a somebody, we realize we were made to have all those things, that we can 'be', live fully, and express ourselves! You have always been a somebody, Brave Front; you just never knew it. But I know it! And I think you are ready to live it now."

This dear child reaches her hands into her heart and pulls out those dead leaves from the dry cracked earth of her being. She lays them in his big hands and looks at him with beseeching eyes. "This is all that I am and all that I own, Mister. Just these dead things in this dead ground. Look!"

I peer over Jesus's shoulder to see them. I know they look lifeless and dried out, but I quickly realize they are not simply dead leaves; they are bulbs. Admittedly, they are in poor shape with no evidence of roots and only old, dried-up leaves, but if they are bulbs then there is surely hope for them! Bulbs can look dead during the winter season, but come spring they resurrect into glorious new life.

The peace pipe is laid to one side, no longer needed for the interview. Instead, Jesus tends this wee child's inner garden. With kindness and assurance, he starts to work on her soil, explaining that he needs to add goodness compost and nourishing slow-release food pellets, and most important of all, water! He calls this water "approval water," for her soil has been crying out for it for so long, and it is the only thing that will bring her land back to life.

He teases the dead leaves off the bulbs and then plants them back into her heart. "You're going to need to let me water these plants every day, sweetheart, and I promise you, you have the makings of a very good garden here!"

Brave Front looks happy. The thought of Jesus spending time with her each day to tend the garden of her heart fills her with such joy.

Jesus chatters away with the child as he works on her garden. His words are like a love song to her heart. She drinks them in as if she can't get enough of them, as if they are the coziest, softest, and warmest of blankets being wrapped around her. As he talks, he paints a picture in her mind of all the flowers that will grow there. She sees how, when the time comes, she will be able to pick those flowers and offer them to others to comfort their souls and help them in difficult times. Some of her flowers will be prayers; no effort involved, just existing as simple prayers.

Jesus plants a creeping peace plant, explaining that it is a spreading ground cover that will have tiny pink flowers and is designed to be invasive. It will carpet her inner garden and reach to every corner of her heart with its restful peace. Looking drunk with wonder, she sighs with contentment. She can already feel the new life moving around inside her heart—creeping, growing, deepening, rising.

Finally, Jesus lifts his gorgeous feathered headdress and places it ceremoniously on Brave Front's head. It is truly magnificent! She smiles and giggles as he explains that she is like him and that what she feels, thinks, and says is important. His authority is her authority. Not like a power that dominates and controls other people, diminishing and abusing them (as she was once treated when she lived in the desolate, open spaces) but more like a power that raises others up to be equals, recognizing the value in each one, noticing the state of the flowers and soil in their hearts and tending their gardens just like he has done hers.

This precious child embraces the validity of his words without a doubt in her mind. She has no sense that she will have to strive to make them happen. Instead, she has a deep-rooted sensation that they are who she is becoming, even who she has become! She knows now that she exists and that she is a somebody. She has lived her life as a sacrifice and as protector for her twin sister, Traumatized One. That ends now. These two Little Fi's have finally been freed from that which imprisoned and limited them, and they are fully alive.

As I write the final words for the story of Brave Front, I remember another of David Hayward's drawings of Sophia. He named it *Angel*, and her wings look almost like the feathered headdress that Jesus presented to my Little Fi.

David describes this drawing as his favourite picture of his truest self. This set-free "Sophia" (our inner wisdom) brings such beauty to the world. He quotes Marianne Williamson from *A Return to Love*: "We are born to make manifest the glory of God that is within us. It is not just in some of us. It is in everyone. And as we let our light shine, we give other people permission to do the same. As we are liberated from our own fear, our presence automatically liberates others."

Brave Front has become so beautiful, and she has grown to be woman. Perhaps her headdress is more than a ceremonial piece depicting mastery, authority, and wisdom. Perhaps it encapsulates something of her new life, for she will not only walk free but one day may rise up and fly.

Angel, with the kind permission of David Hayward

Part 3
AFTERTHOUGHTS

The Great Allower and the Great Co-Sufferer

For many years I had a big issue with God. Why had he allowed the events of my childhood? This question was like a massive boulder that weighed on my thoughts, blocked my vision, and stunted my growth. Over time I began to realize that it had become unhelpful to me and that it was actually preventing healing from happening. I realized that God was asking me to shelve the question, to set it aside unanswered for the time being, so we could make some progress together on the pain I was carrying. Obviously, this took a measure of trust on my part, but God has never forbidden the question or tried to take it away from me. The question was perfectly valid; it was just that I wasn't ready or able to recognize the answer yet.

Sometimes people have expressed the view to me that God never puts us through more than we can bear, thinking this would be a comfort. Such a sentiment has always been intolerable to me and causes all that is in me (no doubt my inner children in particular) to recoil and run for the hills or, alternatively, to want to vomit. I simply cannot accept it. Firstly, I don't believe that God controls me or the people and circumstances in my life like a grand (albeit loving) puppeteer. Therefore, I don't see him as the author of all that happens to me. Second, such a view invalidates the experiences of my Little Ones by suggesting that they have not suffered enough to "go under." My childhood was what it was, my formative years were damaging and too much for my young self to handle, and I do not believe God would wish that on any child. Certainly, he would never orchestrate it.

In more recent years I read Richard Rohr's book, *Immortal Diamond*. My one lasting takeaway from his writing was the page in which he described God as the "Great Allower." It stuck to me like glue. Here is an extract.

> God is the Great Allower, despite all the attempts of ego, culture and even religion to prevent God from allowing. Show me where God does not allow. God lets women be raped and raped women conceive, God lets tyrants succeed and God lets me make my own mistakes again and again. He does not enforce his own commandments... God's total allowing of everything has in fact become humanity's major complaint. If we were truly being honest, God is both a scandal and a supreme disappointment to most of us. We would prefer a God of domination and control to a God of allowing, as most official prayers make clear.

"Great Allower" is a frightening and uncomfortable name for God because it confronts us with the reality of how difficult or even horrific life can be. It also contradicts our religious hopes and requirements of any God we would want to pledge allegiance to. But for me it sits well with my Little Ones because it means they don't have to pretend that bad stuff didn't happen to them or that it didn't deeply wound them or that it wasn't too much to bear. God allowed all that trauma to happen.

Thankfully, there is more to the story of a God who allows all manner of things, for this God who loves unconditionally and freely has promised to be with us at all times no matter what we are going through and no matter who we are. I know this will not satisfy many people, but for me it has become enough. The relentless "withness" of Great Love is my true consolation. This withness (our beloved Emmanuel) cherishes us, roots for us, believes in us, advocates for us, holds us, strengthens us, encourages us, and never, ever abandons us. The trick in the highs and lows of life is to come to know this and to recognize the signs of its truth all around us! That was the gift that Listening Prayer gave to me. I got to "see" the withness of Jesus and how deeply he cared (and had always cared) for my broken parts.

I no longer crave an answer to the question, "Why?" I recognize that the freedom that I have to violate others' boundaries and needs is the same freedom that everyone else is given. Unfortunate and wicked stuff happens to the innocent and the guilty. The better question, in my opinion, is, "Where was God when it was happening?"

During my teens, twenties, and thirties, whenever I tried to picture where God was in relation to my childhood, he always looked like a businessman with a briefcase at his side sitting in the armchair in my bedroom. The word I would use to describe him was "indifferent." He was so detached from my suffering and sadness that it was obvious he didn't care. This was a God who had other more important people to be with than me and who was unaffected by my plight. I had a strong faith in God and put so much effort into being a good Christian, but we had never truly connected.

Another confusing element to my first decades of faith was that I had no real understanding of what love was. I knew that "God is love" (1 John 4:8), but I didn't know what that actually looked like or, more importantly, what it *didn't* look like. Love was a polluted word in my life, spoiled by all the cruel and manipulative things done in its name. God's seeming indifference toward me and my perception of his unpredictable scary love nature were the double whammy that hindered my recovery process.

I had always felt like I'd been left out. Others had wonderful experiences of God's help but not me. I figured I just was not lovable enough or good enough; I was not one of his preferred children. That feeling of exclusion from the club of favoured believers added to my sense of rejection. I could only watch from what I called "the other side of the garden fence" as God helped and blessed others. When I began to practice Listening Prayer and met with Jesus, giving him access to me through my imagination, it was mind-boggling to discover what sort of person he really was. He demonstrated extraordinary kindness to me in ways I had only dreamed that love could be. It turned out he was far from indifferent and unaffected by my suffering. In fact, I often saw him cry with my Little Ones, and he used any means possible to reach them. None of them were too far gone or too grotesque for him to cherish. It was then I came to understand him as the Great Co-Sufferer. Their suffering was his suffering, and he was hell bent on bringing them comfort.

Listening Prayer finally started to answer the question of where God was. As my heart healed, I came to realize that he had been with me all along, right in the thick of the trauma and pain. This changed everything; in fact, it changed my life. God is not only the Great Allower, he is also the Great Co-Sufferer. I know now that God will allow even the unimaginable to happen to us but that this is not a reflection of how little he loves us. The choices, beautiful and ugly, of every human are always honoured. But I also know that he will be with us through it all, not as a bystander looking on or as a dispassionate far-off deity but as a dear friend and soulmate, traveling to the depths with us, tending our hearts, holding us close, and offering comfort and healing.

Trauma and Listening Prayer

A concern that is guaranteed to be raised whenever I participate in offering any Listening Prayer training is that we surely risk retraumatizing clients if we address their trauma in a healing session. This is a perfectly valid concern and may well be born out of experience with other prayer and counseling ministries administered by laypeople.

When I was writing this book, I was very aware that I didn't want to traumatize any of my readers in the telling of my stories. I am highly sensitive myself and easily shaken up by other people's suffering. I hope I have not added to your distress in any way.

Listening Prayer is beautifully tailored to the needs of the traumatized. Some folks can think of a memory, picture it in their imagination, and then invite Jesus (or whomever represents Great Love to them) into it. But for others, like me, the memories are too painful to return to, and to do so would feel more damaging and destabilizing. In such cases we ask God for a new, safe place for us to meet with Jesus. This works perfectly! The same issues can be taken care of as in the memory but without having to revisit the place of the trauma. It is far easier to be healed in a "safe place" because there we will feel protected enough to open ourselves and be vulnerable to what love has to offer.

Additionally, Jesus often has a roundabout way of healing us from trauma. To make it more comforting and less distressing for us, he does not insist we face it head on. Instead, with extraordinary wisdom he chooses a path that may seem so painless that we almost don't realize we're being led along healing steps. We might fear that without pain there is no gain! It requires trust to follow where he is leading us in our imagination during Listening Prayer and to accept that something so seemingly simple might even rewire our brains. Yet, again and again I have seen deep, lasting healing come for exquisitely debilitating trauma by simple, almost playful, dialogue and exchange with the Living Christ.

Comments on Listening Prayer: Eden Jersak

One of the great privileges of my life is in having been a part of this story. If the only fruit of Listening Prayer was Fi's miraculous healing, that would have been enough, but honestly, there are great clusters of fruit from this ministry!

Listening Prayer is such an amazing tool to use in healing memories and trauma. It is simple and straightforward and can be used for as little as a few short minutes or stretch into years, as Fi's story did. It is extremely important that the person receiving and engaging in Listening Prayer is a willing participant. The magnitude of Fi's healing was a reflection of her willingness to engage in the process. The outcomes that Fi experienced would not have been nearly as extraordinary if she had not engaged her will. Jesus will not force us into healing if we don't want to take part in it!

We did have occasions when well-intentioned parents, friends, and spouses would call and ask us to do Listening Prayer with their loved ones. We always asked that the person who would be participating in the prayer would call us back and engage in a short conversation. We would come to a point in the conversation where we would ask, "Do you want to be healed?" If the answer was anything less than a straightforward "YES!", we would back off. Not everyone wants to be healed or feels they need healing, and so until they say, "Yes," there is little point.

There was a situation once where someone flew their daughter in to "get some" Listening Prayer. We were prepared for this to take a couple of days, but there was absolutely no path forward with this woman. It was confusing, and, try as we might, she just could not hear or see anything. Suddenly, it dawned on Brad to ask, "Do you want to be healed?" Her answer was "No!" It was then that we understood the need for the will to be fully engaged in Listening Prayer.

For those who have a lifetime of trauma and abuse, the mountain can seem far too big to climb, but I would encourage you not to try to scale the mountain by climbing straight up the face. Rather, follow well-used trails, use switchbacks, and travel as lightly as possible. As you are able, rid yourself of judgements, unforgiveness, burdens, and anything else that will weigh you down. The lighter you travel, the further you can go.

As you climb, you will reach vistas where you can look back and see how far and high you have come. Take your time at these viewpoints—sit down, have a rest, look in all directions, and consider how things have changed and what new things you can see. These stops along the way are what give you the strength and inspiration to continue on. Listening Prayer is not a race; it's a journey.

If your story is not as devastating as Fi's, but you know you need healing just the same, Listening Prayer is still for you. Any little thing that causes us harm, either self-inflicted or caused by others, can be cared for with Listening

Prayer. We practiced Listening Prayer with our three boys as soon as they could speak and communicate what they needed and what they were seeing. We used it with them to address bad dreams, to settle heartaches, and to lift burdens. They each had a few different meeting places where they would engage with Jesus. In teaching children how to engage in Listening Prayer, you are creating a path for them that doesn't have them piling up their pain and trauma but has them bringing their pain to Jesus as it happens. This is a profound life skill!

This journey to healing that Fi has shared is absolutely true and was just as amazing in the moment as it is to read about now. The healing that Fi received has been long lasting and profound to witness. When I recall my first encounter with Fi and compare it to the woman I know now, I still can hardly believe the transformation that has occurred. It is similar to what it would be like to watch a person regrow a limb. To see her living in the fullness of who she was created to be is always inspiring.

Eden Jersak (2021)

COMMENTS ON LISTENING PRAYER: LORIE MARTIN

Being with Fiona through these years of healing is by far one of the greatest highlights of my life. Her determination, resilience, and healing were astonishing. Each breath and moment were sacred encounters with the Living Christ in each unsettled and triggering place of her unconscious wounds and traumas. Accompanying Fi, and her Little Ones, in her gospel (Good News) stories was full of the Guiding Spirit, who is the Healer and Restorer of all things. I truly wish this experience for every person in some way.

Connecting with the Divine and our true self in loving union brings forth the fruit of truth and freedom, which begin as tiny seeds of faith and trust. God's love grows and nurtures us. How God moves in healing ways is truly a mystery, even as God is Mystery. We were made for this beautiful relationship and encounters of divine grace. At times on my own healing journey, it seems to be a full-time job to stay open to grace, "the uncreated energy of God's loving kindness and redeeming love" that stirs and dwells and transforms us from within. Even the openness to grace is grace. Love, prayer, and healing are *all* grace.

That God allows, co-suffers, and indwells us is the most true and authentic way of facing real pain and suffering. Surrendering to this beauty-full God makes a way for beauty to come from the ashes of our lives. It will not help or heal us if we spiritually bypass our experiences with pat answers or religious formulas. It is not ours to go digging around inside our unconscious but to open to the Gracious One who accompanies us in these tender and hidden places at the right time when the safe container and companions are available.

Listening Prayer is a prayerful spiritual practice that creates a venue for interaction with God that can be tested and trusted. I have experienced and witnessed hundreds of life-changing transformations through Listening Prayer. I continue to encourage facilitation and training of this ministry for the healing of people everywhere and for ongoing, deepening, and satisfying friendship with God, however God is known to each one. Nothing could be more satisfying.

What is hidden cannot be healed. "Whatever is not transformed is transmitted," says Franciscan Father Richard Rohr. However, what is transformed is also transmitted. We witness this in Fiona's life as she shares her remarkable story and this healing path with many other people. I celebrate her life, her journey, and her call to love and serve many in their healing experiences.

"But thanks be to God, who . . . through us spreads in every place the fragrance that comes from knowing him . . . a fragrance from life to life." (2 Cor. 2:14–16)

Lorie Martin (2021)

Epilogue

The year 2021 has been a monumental one for me. It is the year of my divorce (after twenty-five years of marriage), the year my two sons flew from the nest, and the year that I finally sat down to write my book. I also find myself involuntarily strapped to the conveyor belt of time as I cling to the last months of my fifties and brace myself for the next decade. My dear body, which has served me so well for so long, is starting to show signs of sag, spread, wrinkles, and slowing down. It feels like a lot is changing in a short space of time, and it has been a bit of a bumpy ride!

What I have noticed about all these changes in my life is that each one seems to lean into my tendency to feel shame about who and what I am. Shame has been the bedrock of my life (I am a 2 on the enneagram), and I can identify it's mark on me from my earliest days. My wise old head tells me it's ridiculous to feel ashamed of my failed marriage, my children's need to move away, my aging body, and my less than perfect writing skills. What I want is to embrace all of these things wholeheartedly, just as they are--without judgement and definitely without shame! But there remains an ugly trace of embarrassment that casts its shadow across my thinking and will not let go.

As I have grappled with the prospect of publishing my book and allowing others to read my stories and get to "know" Fi, I turned to Listening Prayer once again (as is my practice when needed) and asked Katherine Murray if she would facilitate a session for me in the spring of this year to help me tackle my internal shame dialogue once again. Katherine is a trusted, experienced woman who not only trains others to facilitate Listening Prayer but also heads up the Listening Prayer ministry at St. Dunstan's Anglican Church in Aldergrove, BC.

I know enough about life to know that, by and large, our "issues" are not resolved in any single one-off healing event. Instead, those weaknesses invite us into a process. If we accept this journey, this multifaceted way of healing, we will find that we are given the opportunity for honest awareness, significant encounters, and eureka moments. We are invited to seek help and also to find uncomfortable resting places where, if we are brave, we might come to peace with our inability to effect change within ourselves. Great Love accompanies us, even guides us, and somehow all these messy components bring us ever nearer to self-acceptance and wholeness. Our destination, it turns out, is nowhere near as important as the journey! But you knew that already, I'm sure. So, although I cannot say that I will live shamelessly from here on out, my Listening Prayer session was still touching, enlightening, and impactful and will undoubtedly move me forward in the right direction. I would like to share it with you now as my final story. Don't forget that it comes many years after all the other stories you have just read and that though it draws this small book to a close, my own journey, like yours, continues on and always will.

* * *

We meet under a large dogwood tree at the edge of the meadow. Little Ones, dressed in loose white cottons and comfy linens, follow me there like a stream of ducklings behind their mother. They march along, full of lively joy and chatter, wading through the long grass and picking flowers along the way. The dogwood is beautiful. She is covered in a bridal veil of soft creamy flowers whose large petals spoon the sunlight. How tall and upright she stands, providing shade and a lovely visual carnival for our senses.

Jesus greets us all with warm hugs and kisses; our reunion is sweet and full of giggles and laughter. All my Little Ones press in around him and could easily smother him with their loving affection. Our faces glow with delight at our chance for a visit. He is such a dear, dear friend.

When asked why he chose for us to meet under this wonderful tree, he shrugs and, with a smile, says, "Because I know you love the dogwood Fi--what gives you joy, gives me joy too. And besides, it reminds me of you, Sweet Fi! You are just like this dogwood; upright and beautiful and without blemish!" I grin back at him. It is impossible to outdo his generosity. He really is the best!

Today is an important day, and Jesus has an agenda for me as I have asked him to help me with the vestiges of my difficult foundations of shame. He carries a quiet air of confidence and reassurance as he leads me along the path toward the far corner of the meadow. My Little Ones follow as we amble along. Soon we reach the entrance to my cave—I didn't know it could be accessed from the field. Perhaps it has been here all along. I have stood in front of this cave so many times, and I have entered it on occasion, with the help of this kind man at my side. It no longer holds the same terror and dread it once did, but today I am not at all keen to submerge myself in its cold, damp darkness. I have been imagining my shame as an underground monster that erupts unexpectedly from the depths, an opportunistic predator intent on devouring me. If this is what I'll get to meet in my cave, then I am not looking forward to it! I ask Jesus if we can leave my Little Ones to play in the meadow with the angels, as I do not want them to be scared or traumatized. Jesus agrees, and they run off to play without a care in the world.

Jesus is always in tune with my emotions. He knows me better than I know myself, and he has a way of encouraging me that always honours my choices, validates my feelings, and yet invites me toward health and healing. He lets me look into his face now to show me that he has absolutely no fear, not an ounce, not a drop. "It's going to be alright, pet lamb," he says (a term of affection my father used to use). He gently coaxes me, holding up a glowing lantern that will light our path in the darkness that awaits.

And so we step into the inky black, and I find myself walking behind him along an underground passageway. He holds out the light in front of him, his other arm reaching behind for me to grasp. He will never let go of me. This is something we are going to do together, and I know I can trust him.

Before long I notice that the walls and floor of this passageway are sparkling with gems of every colour, with shiny gold and silver metals. Not just the walls themselves but the whole pathway is strewn with treasures, piled high on each side! This is not at all what I was expecting! Oh my goodness, this is a corridor lined with what reminds me of fairy-tale pirate booty or the exquisite ornaments of a pharaoh's burial chamber, throwing glowing and dazzling lights in every direction, reflected from the light of the lamp.

How come there's so much wealth? Why is it so bright and glittery?

Jesus smiles. "This is because so much is already healed and taken care of. These are all symbols of a great redemption!" His eyes twinkle as he explains. It's true; we have taken care of so much that was once hidden in the darkness of my cave, and it really has become treasure!

The passageway leads shortly to an underground cavern in which I discover a pool of the most beautiful, crystal-clear waters. Jesus invites me to drink, so I can be deeply refreshed. We pause for a few moments to rest and prepare.

Now we must travel deeper into the earth, and the way through is becoming narrower. There are no treasures down here, just the dark red-brown earth packed underfoot and roughly cut up the sides. At times Jesus must turn sideways to pass through where the walls press in, but he does not let go of my hand, and his lantern is still burning brightly ahead of us. I can smell the soil now. This is the earth's domain, and her scent is pungent and undiluted by all that is carried in the air up there at the surface. She is deeply stable, timeless. Jesus tells me this route is very familiar to him, though it is new to me. It is his feet that have worn this pathway. His footprints are embedded in the ground under my feet, for he has walked it so many, many times.

My imagination ignites as we continue to walk. I picture a terrifying dragon of shame awaiting us at the end of the passageway, and I hope rather desperately that Jesus has brought his sword with him. Perhaps he can slay this thing once and for all!

Jesus turns and sits down before me, inviting me to join him on this good and faithful earth. "What if what lies ahead is not waiting to consume you, Fi, but is waiting to be freed?" I ponder what he's saying, somewhat puzzled at the suggestion that there might be a monster for us to free rather than to destroy. "Have courage, sweetheart," he says, wiping a tear from my cheek. He places his hand over my heart to transfer to me some of what makes him so brave. Then he holds my head gently in his dear hands and prays a blessing on my overactive, fear-filled imagination. When I am ready, he helps me up, and we continue on.

At some point the pathway turns into a long set of steps that fall away into the depths. I am grateful for the railing on the wall. We follow the stairs down, down, down until eventually we reach an old wooden doorway blocking our path. I sense that the name of the door is "Opportunity." We stand on the small landing while I try to muster the courage to let Jesus open the ancient door. He has a beautiful key with which to unlock it, one of his favourites, apparently. He tells me it had to be this lovely to be worthy of this particular door, for it is so special.

I finally agree that we will proceed, and he allows me to keep my eyes squeezed shut, as if blindfolded, as he opens the door and leads me through. I brace myself for the dragon.

My first impression under my toes is that I'm on a beach. Can this be right? But when I open my eyes, warm white sand stretches before me in a gentle curve around a stunning tropical bay: turquoise waters lapping gently on an unspoiled beach and palm trees bending gracefully toward the ocean.

Jesus is beaming. "This, my Dear Fi, is the place of your core. See how peaceful and lovely you are?" I guess he's smiling at my amazement and the wonder on my face. Such a restful place! So idyllic! There are definitely no dragons here! I can't take it in; it's not at all what I had anticipated. I don't know what to say or what to think.

There may be no dragons here, but there are many dragonflies, their bodies encrusted with gems of iridescent harmonies and their wings so delicately veined. Such gentle, humble creatures. A whole swarm of them gather in front of us, hovering and beckoning us to follow them. I look to Jesus to check that I'm getting this right. He nods and smiles some more, and we step toward this vision of a moving cloud as they lead us along the beach. I'm in heaven! The warm sunshine on my arms and face, the soft sand under my feet, those extraordinary beings ahead of me, and the stunning waterfront to my right. I drink the air like a hummingbird drinks nectar, recognizing how life-giving every breath is, not just to my body but also to everything that is in me.

The excitement of the dragonflies is escalating, their vibrations too joyful to be contained. Before we even get there, I can see where they are taking me. There is a sheltered spot at a small rocky outcrop ahead, and lying in the cleft is a baby, small and perfect, wrapped loosely in sacking and happily kicking her little legs and arms. This wee infant is not at all neglected or flawed. She has been taken care of by Mother Nature and all the creatures of her kingdom. The dragonflies say she is a daughter waiting to be claimed and that their time of looking after her is complete, for now it is my turn to care for her. They present her to me as my daughter, and they tell me she a child of promise!

A daughter? My daughter? I have sons, but I never had a girl. Am I really to be this baby's mother?

They tell me that this baby is without shame and that she has been hidden here at the core of my being until it was safe for us to be reunited. A long, long time ago she was snatched from the flames, rescued from danger and whisked away in the nick of time without even the smell of smoke on her skin. She doesn't have my history, and she didn't experience what I did, which is why she is completely free of shame. It has simply never touched her.

As I stand there trying to take it all in and longing to hold my new daughter, I sense my Little Ones in the meadow far away, and I feel their excitement at this new member who will be joining our family. They cannot wait to see her, to hold her, and to love her.

I experience a wonderful feeling of homecoming as I take her into my arms and behold her. How perfectly we are suited! How comfortable she is with me. Her lack of shame will be imparted to me as she grows in my nurturing. Jesus radiates joy. Mother (shamed)-self and daughter (shameless)-self have finally come together after so many decades apart. The dragonflies dance riotously as they encircle us, the whole beach sighs, the trees hum, and the baby nuzzles into me. Jesus says we will never be parted from each other. I am what she needs to be able to grow up, and she is what I need in order to fully heal. I thank Mother Nature for caring for her. Nature has been my friend and inspiration for as long as I can remember, but I never knew she was taking care of my secret daughter alongside her work of so generously strengthening and supporting me.

We leave this idyllic place in a small boat: Jesus, me, and my daughter of promise. The dragonflies push us out to sea, and the waters carry us with such great care, steering us gently on our journey back to a small pebbly beach just below the meadow. The Little Ones have already come racing down the stony pathway to greet us as we arrive, their joy spilling from them in sparkling giggles and little bursts of clapping. I hold up my daughter for them to see, her eyes large as she looks at all these adoring children whose hearts have already fully embraced her. She drinks it all in, absorbing it into her being without question or hesitation. The Little Ones lead us up the pathway, back to the dogwood tree where we sit and regroup for a short while. Jesus kisses my head and tells me how proud he is of me; he knew I was ready for all this. He blesses my wee daughter, she who will fulfil her destiny. She smiles and gurgles up at him.

Finally, I rest myself back against the trunk of the lovely tree, snuggling my sleepy daughter into my neck while my Little Ones run off with Jesus to play tag in the meadow. It has been a day of surprises, all of them pleasant! I had no idea that there was any part of me that wasn't tainted by shame, since it's influence had begun even while I was in the womb. I feel full of gratitude and wonder to meet her and to be reunited with this part of myself. What an honour that I am the one tasked with loving her and raising her! Gaining a daughter feels extraordinary. Even our landing at the pebble beach impacted me, for my infant daughter had no fear or shame at meeting new people, no unhealthy self-consciousness or reticence. Instead, she was open and welcomed my Little Ones immediately into her heart, remaining present in the moment and positive about the possibilities that lay ahead. I wish I could be like her! And perhaps now I really have a chance of being that!

F. T. Davidson
whenalittleonehums@gmail.com

Printed in Great Britain
by Amazon